ARCHIBALD HF

CW00801235

# ASSYRIA

## ITS PRINCES, PRIESTS AND PEOPLE

Elibron Classics
www.elibron.com

Elibron Classics series.

© 2005 Adamant Media Corporation.

ISBN 1-4021-5562-X (paperback)
ISBN 1-4021-5561-1 (hardcover)

This Elibron Classics Replica Edition is an unabridged facsimile
of the edition published in 1885 by the Religious Tract Society,
London.

Elibron and Elibron Classics are trademarks of
Adamant Media Corporation. All rights reserved.

This book is an accurate reproduction of the original. Any marks, names, colophons, imprints, logos or other symbols or identifiers that appear on or in this book, except for those of Adamant Media Corporation and BookSurge, LLC, are used only for historical reference and accuracy and are not meant to designate origin or imply any sponsorship by or license from any third party.

MONOLITH OF SHALMANESER II.

*(From the original in the British Museum.)*

By-Paths of Bible Knowledge.
VII.

# ASSYRIA

## ITS PRINCES, PRIESTS, AND PEOPLE.

BY

## A. H. SAYCE, M.A.

DEPUTY PROFESSOR OF COMPARATIVE PHILOLOGY, OXFORD, HON. LL.D. DUBLIN, ETC.

AUTHOR OF 'FRESH LIGHT FROM THE ANCIENT MONUMENTS,' 'AN INTRODUCTION
TO EZRA, NEHEMIAH, AND ESTHER,' ETC.

LONDON:

THE RELIGIOUS TRACT SOCIETY,

56, PATERNOSTER ROW, 65, ST. PAUL'S CHURCHYARD,
AND 164, PICCADILLY.

1885.

# CONTENTS.

———•———

## CHAPTER I.

# ILLUSTRATIONS.

———✦———

# PREFACE.

AMONG the many wonderful achievements of the present century there is none more wonderful than the recovery and decipherment of the monuments of ancient Nineveh. For generations the great oppressing city had slept buried beneath the fragments of its own ruins, its history lost, its very site forgotten. Its name had passed into the region of myth even in the age of the classical writers of Greece and Rome; Ninos or Nineveh had become a hero-king about whom strange legends were told, and whose conquests were fabled to have extended from the Mediterranean to India. Little was known of the history of the mighty Assyrian Empire beyond what might be learnt from the Old Testament, and that little was involved in doubt and obscurity. Scholars wrote long treatises to reconcile the statements of Greek historians with those of Scripture, but they only succeeded in evolving theories which were contradicted and overthrown by the next writer. There was none so bold as to suggest that the history and life of Assyria were still lying hidden beneath the ground, ready to rise up and disclose their secrets at the touch of a magician's rod. The rod was the spade and the patient sagacity which

deciphered and interpreted what the spade had found.
It might have been thought that the cuneiform or wedge-
shaped inscriptions of Assyria could never be forced to
reveal their mysteries. The language in which they
were written was unknown, and all clue to the meaning
of the multitudinous characters that composed them had
long been lost. No bilingual text came to the aid of the
decipherer like the Rosetta Stone, whose Greek inscription had furnished the key to the meaning of the
Egyptian hieroglyphics. Nevertheless the great feat
was accomplished. Step by step the signification of the
cuneiform characters and the words they concealed was
made out, until it is now possible to translate an ordinary
Assyrian text with as much ease and certainty as a page
of the Old Testament.

And the revelation that awaited the decipherer was
startling in the extreme. The ruins of Nineveh yielded
not only sculptures and inscriptions carved in stone, but
a whole library of books. True, the books are written
upon clay, and not on paper, but they are none the less
real books, dealing with all the subjects of knowledge
known at the time they were compiled, and presenting
us with a clear and truthful reflection of Assyrian
thought and belief. We can not only trace the architectural plans of the Assyrian palaces, and study the
bas-reliefs in which the Assyrians have pictured themselves and the life they led; we can also penetrate to
their inmost thoughts and feelings, and read their history
as they have told it themselves.

It is a strange thing to examine for the first time one of the clay tablets of the old Assyrian library. Usually it has been more or less broken by the catastrophe of that terrible day when Nineveh was captured by its enemies, and the palace and library burnt and destroyed together. But whether it is a fragment or a complete tablet, it is impossible not to handle it reverently when cleaning it from the dirt with which its long sojourn in the earth has encrusted it, and spelling out its words for the first time for more than 2,000 years. When last the characters upon it were read, it was in days when Assyria was still a name of terror, and the destruction that God's prophets had predicted was still to come. When its last reader laid it aside, Judah had not as yet undergone the chastisement of the Babylonish exile, the Old Testament was an uncompleted volume, the kingdom of the Messiah a promise of the distant future. We are brought face to face, as it were, with men who were the contemporaries of Isaiah, of Hezekiah, of Ahaz; nay, of men whose names have been familiar to us since we first read the Bible by our mother's side.

Tiglath-Pileser and Sennacherib can never again be to us mere names. We possess the records which they caused to be written, and in which they told the story of their campaigns in Palestine. The records are not copies of older texts, with all the errors that human fallibility causes copyists and scribes to make. They are the original documents which were recited to the kings who ordered them to be compiled, and who may have held

them in their own hands.   The gulf of centuries and
forgetfulness that has divided us from Sennacherib is
filled up when we read the account of his invasion of
Judah, which seems to come from his own lips.   Never
again can the heroes of the Old Testament be to us as
lay-figures, whose story is told by a voice that comes
from a dark and unreal past.   The voice is now become
a living one, and we can realise that Isaiah and those of
whom Isaiah wrote were men of flesh and blood like
ourselves, with the same passions, the same needs, the
same temptations.

This realisation of Old Testament history is not the
only result of the recovery of Assyria upon Biblical
studies.   It is a very important result, but there are
others besides of equal importance.   One of these is the
unexpected confirmation of the correctness of Holy Writ
which Assyrian discovery has afforded.   The later history of the Old Testament no longer stands alone.   Once
it was itself the sole witness for the truth of the narra
tives it contains.   Classical history or legend dealt with
other lands and other ages; there were no documents
besides those contained in the Old Testament to which
we could appeal in support of its statements.   All is
changed now.   The earth has yielded up its secrets; the
ancient civilisation of Assyria has stepped forth again
into the light of day, and has furnished us with records,
the authenticity of which none can deny, which run side
by side with those of the Books of Kings, confirming,
explaining, and illustrating them.   It has been said that

just at the moment when sceptical criticism seemed to
have achieved its worst, and to have resolved the narratives of the Old Testament into myths or fables, God's
Providence was raising up from the grave of centuries a
new and unimpeachable witness for their truth. Indeed,
so strikingly was this the case, that one of the objections
brought against the correctness of Assyrian decipherment in its early days was that Assyrian monarchs could
never have concerned themselves with petty kingdoms
like those of Samaria and Judah, as the decipherers made
them do. Before the cuneiform monuments were interpreted, no one could have suspected that they would
have poured such a flood of light upon Old Testament
history.

This light is manifold. The very language of the
inscriptions has helped to explain difficult passages in
the Hebrew Bible. Assyrian turns out to be very closely
related to Hebrew, as closely related, in fact, as two
strongly marked English dialects are to one another.
There is no other Semitic language (except, of course,
Phœnician, which is practically the same as Hebrew)
which is so nearly allied to it. And thanks to the
library of Nineveh, and its lexicons and lists of synonymous words, we have a larger literature, and a larger
vocabulary, to draw upon in the case of Assyrian than
we have in the case of Hebrew. The consequence is
that Assyrian may sometimes settle the meaning of a
word which occurs only once or very rarely in the Old
Testament. Thus the word *z'bhûl*, which Hebrew

scholars had supposed to mean 'a dwelling,' is shown
by the Assyrian texts to signify a 'height,' so that in
1 Kings viii. 13, Solomon does not declare to God that
he had built Him 'an house to dwell in,' as the
Authorised Version renders the passage, but 'a lofty
temple.'    Naturally words of Assyrian origin, like Rab-
shakeh and Tartan, have first received their explanation
from the decipherment of the Assyrian inscriptions.
They are not proper names, but titles, the Rab-shakeh
being 'the chief of the princes,' or Vizier, and the
Tartan, the commander-in-chief.

But not only do we find parallels to Hebrew in the
individual words of Assyrian, we also find  parallel
expressions which illustrate and explain those of the
Hebrew text.   We all remember the statement that the
'Lord rained upon Sodom and upon Gomorrah brim-
stone and fire from the Lord out of heaven.'   The
same phrase occurs in an unpublished Accadian hymn
addressed to a deity whose name is lost, but who was
probably Rimmon the Air-god.   The Accadian original
describes him as 'raining fire and stones upon the
enemy,' which the Assyrian translation changes into
'raining stones and fire upon the foe' in exact confor-
mity with the Hebrew phrase.   The familiar expression
'the Lord of Hosts,' similarly finds its analogue and illustration in the common Assyrian title of the supreme god
Assur: 'lord of the legions of heaven and earth,' these
legions being the multitudinous spirits and angels whose
home was in 'the heaven above and the earth below.'

We can hardly speak here of the accounts of the Creation, the Deluge, and the Tower of Babel, to which Mr. George Smith gave the name of 'the Chaldean Genesis,' and which agree so closely with the corresponding accounts in the Hebrew Book of Genesis. Though found in the library of Nineveh, they are really copies of older Babylonian works, and therefore belong rather to Babylonian than to Assyrian history. It is only the account of the Creation in six days which may perhaps be of purely Assyrian origin. What a resemblance it offers to the first chapter of Genesis will be seen from the extracts from it in the chapter on Assyrian Religion.

It is in the domain of history that the light cast upon Old Testament Scripture by Assyrian research has been fullest and strongest. No one can read the sketch of Assyrian history as revealed by the monuments which is given in the following pages, without perceiving how important it is for the proper understanding of the ancient Scriptures. For the first time the prophecies in Isaiah which refer to a capture of Jerusalem receive their explanation, and the sceptical criticism is answered which found in them a prediction of events that never took place. The chapter in which Isaiah describes the onward march of the Assyrian host against Jerusalem (ch. x.) is no 'ideal' description of 'an ideal campaign,' the verses in which he tells us of the sufferings endured by the beleaguered inhabitants of the Jewish capital (ch. xxii.) are no 'exaggerated account of a possible

catastrophe,' the prophecies in which he declares that
the devoted city was about to fall into the hands of its
enemies (x. 34, xxii. 14) were not unfulfilled threats.
We learn from the inscriptions of Sargon that already,
ten years before the campaign of his son Sennacherib,
the Assyrian monarch had swept through 'the wide-
spread land of Judah,' and had made it a tributary
province.   It was not the army of Sennacherib to which
Isaiah was alluding on the day whereon he declared that
the Assyrian host was at Nob, only a short half-hour to
the north of Jerusalem, but the more terrible veterans of
Sargon who marched against the holy city along the
northern road.   Similar light is thrown by the Assyrian
monuments upon another prophecy of Isaiah, in which
he pronounces the doom upon the land of Egypt
(ch. xix.).   The prophecy has sometimes been referred
by critics to a later age than that of the great prophet;
but the records of Esar-haddon prove that it is strictly
applicable to his time, and to his time only.   The
unexpected revelation they have made to us of the
Assyrian conquest of Egypt, and its division into twenty
vassal satrapies shows us who was the 'cruel lord' and
'fierce king' into whose hands the Egyptians were
given, and paints the picture of an epoch in which 'the
Egyptians' fought 'every one against his brother, and
every one against his neighbour; city against city, and
kingdom against kingdom.'   The Isaianic authorship of
'the burden of Egypt' can never again be denied.

  Nahum, again, we can now read with a new interest

and a new understanding. The very date of his prophecy, so long disputed, can be fixed approximately by
the reference it contains to the sack of No-Amon or
Thebes (iii. 8). The prophecy was delivered hard upon
sixty years before the fall of Nineveh, when the Assyrian
Empire was at the height of its prosperity, and mistress
of the Eastern world. Human foresight could little
have imagined that so great and terrible a power was so
soon to disappear. And yet at the very moment when
it seemed strongest and most secure, the Jewish prophet
was uttering a prediction which the excavations of Botta
and Layard have shown to have been carried out
literally in fact. As we thread our way among the ruins
of Nineveh, or trace the after history of the deserted
and forgotten site, we see everywhere the fulfilment of
Nahum's prophecy. Of the words that he pronounced
against the doomed city, there is none which has not
come to pass.

Those who would learn how marvellously the monuments of Assyria illustrate and corroborate the pages of
sacred history, need only compare the records they
contain with the narratives of the Books of Kings which
relate to the same period. The one complements and
supplies the missing chapters given by the other. The
Bible informs us why Sennacherib left Hezekiah
unpunished, and never despatched another army to
Palestine; the cuneiform annals explain the causes of
his murder, and the reason of the flight of his sons to
Ararat or Armenia. The single passage in Scripture in

which the name of Sargon is mentioned, no longer
remains isolated and unintelligible; we have no longer
any need to identify him with Tiglath-Pileser, or
Shalmaneser, or any other Assyrian prince with whom
the fancy of older commentators confounded him; we
now know that he was one of the most powerful of
Assyrian conquerors, and we have his own independent
testimony to that siege and capture of Ashdod which is
the occasion of the mention of his name in Scripture.
Between the history of the monuments and the history
of the Bible there is perpetual contact; and the voice
of the monuments is found to be in strict harmony with
that of the Old Testament.

Before concluding this Preface, I have to thank Mr.
W. G. Hird for his kindness in undertaking the task of
compiling an Index to the volume.

# CHRONOLOGICAL TABLE OF THE KINGS OF ASSYRIA.

| | B.C. |
|---|---|
| Bel-kapkapi .. ... ... ... ... ... | 1700 (?) |
| Adasi ... .. ... ... ... ... | |
| Bel bani, his son ... ... ... ... ... | 1650 (?) |
| Assur sum esir ... ... ... ... ... | 1600 (?) |
| Adar tiglath-Assuri ... ... ... ... ... | 1600 (?) |
| Irba Rimmon ... ... ... ... . ... | 1550 (?) |
| Assur nadin akhi, his son ... ... ... ... | |
| Assur bel-nisi-su ... ... ... ... *cir.* | 1450 |
| Buyur-Assur ... ... ... ... ... ... | 1420 |
| Assur yuballidh ... ... ... ... ... | 1400 |
| Bel nirari, his son ... ... .. ... ... | 1380 |
| Pudil (Pedael), his son ... ... ... ... | 1350 |
| Rimmon-nirari I, his son ... ... ... ... | 1320 |
| Shalmaneser I, his son ... ... ... ... | 1300 |
| Tiglath-Adar I, his son ... ... ... ... | 1280 |
| Bel kudur utsur (Belchadrezzar), his son ... ... | 1260 |
| Assur-narara and Nebo-dân ... ... ... ... | 1240 |
| Adar-pal-esar (Adar-pileser) ... ... ... ... | 1220 |
| Assur-dân I, his son ... ... ... ... ... | 1200 |
| Mutaggil-Nebo, his son ... ... ... ... | 1180 |
| Assur-ris ilim, his son .. ... ... ... ... | 1160 |
| Tiglath-pileser I, his son ... ... ... ... | 1140 |
| Assur bel kala, his son ... ... ... ... | 1110 |

B C.

| | |
|---|---|
| Samas Rimmon I, his brother . . .. | 1090 |
| Assur rab buri . . . | |
| Assur zalmati . | |
| Assur dân II . . . | 930 |
| Rimmon nirari II, his son | 911 |
| Tiglath Adar II, his son . | 889 |
| Assur natsir pal, his son | 883 |
| Shalmaneser II, his son . | 858 |
| Samas Rimmon II, his son . | 823 |
| Rimmon nirari III, his son | 810 |
| Shalmaneser III ... .. . | 781 |
| Assur-dân III ... . | 771 |
| Assur-nirari ... . . | 753 |
| Pulu (Pul) usurps the throne and founds the 2nd Empire under the name of Tiglath-Pileser II | |
| 12th of Iyyar | 745 |
| Ululâ (Elulæos) of Tinu, usurper, takes the name of Shalmaneser IV . .. ... | 727 |
| Sargon, usurper . . ... . | 722 |
| Sennacherib of Khabigal, his son 12th of Ab | 705 |
| Esar-haddon, his son . . | 681 |
| Assur-bani-pal (Sardanapalos), his son . .. | 668 |
| Assur-etil-ili-yukinni, his son ... . *cir.* | 640 |
| (Bel)-sum-iskun ... . . | |
| Esar-haddon II (Sarakos) ... | |
| Fall of Nineveh . .. . . | 606 (?) |

# TABLE OF BIBLICAL DATES ACCORDING TO THE ASSYRIAN MONUMENTS.

# ASSYRIA:
## ITS PRINCES, PRIESTS, AND PEOPLE.

### CHAPTER I.

#### THE COUNTRY AND PEOPLE.

ASSYRIA was the name given to the district which had
been called 'the land of Assur' by its own inhabitants.
Assur, however, had originally been the name, not of a
country, but of a city founded in remote times on the
western bank of the Tigris, midway between the Greater
and the Lesser Zab.  It was the primitive capital of the
district in which it stood, and to which, accordingly, it
lent its name.  It seems to have been built by a people
who spoke an agglutinative language, like the languages
of the modern Fins and Turks, and who were afterwards
supplanted by the Semitic Assyrians.  The name in
their language probably signified 'water-boundary.'
When the country was occupied by the Semitic Assyrians the name was slightly changed, so as to assume
the form of a word which in Assyrian meant 'gracious.'

It so happened that Assyrian mythology knew of a
deity who represented the firmament, and was addressed

as Sar. The name of Sar came in time to be confused with that of Assur, the divine patron of the Assyrian capital, the result being that Assur signified not only a city and country, but also the supreme deity worshipped by their inhabitants. Assur, in fact, became the divine impersonation of the power and constitution of Assyria, at the same time he was also 'the gracious' god and the primæval firmament of heaven.

Assur, whose ruins are now called Kalah Sherghat, did not always remain the capital of Assyria. Its place was taken by a group of cities some 60 miles to the north, above the Greater Zab, and on the eastern side of the Tigris, namely, Nineveh, Calah, and Dur-Sargon. The foundation of Nineveh, the modern Kouyunjik, probably goes back to as early an age as that of Assur, but it was not until a much later period that it became an important city, and supplanted the older capital of the kingdom. Calah, now called Nimrûd, though built some four centuries before, was not made the seat of royalty until the reigns of Assur-natsir-pal and Shalmaneser II, in the 9th century B C., and Dur-Sargon (the modern Khorsabad), as its name implies, was the creation of Sargon. Instead of Dur-Sargon the Book of Genesis (x. 11) mentions Resen 'between Nineveh and Calah.' The site of Resen has not been identified, though its name has been met with in the Assyrian inscriptions under the form of Res-eni, 'the head of the spring.'

The passage of Genesis in which Resen is referred to

unfortunately admits of a double translation. If we adopt the rendering of the margin, and translate 'out of that land he went forth into Assyria and builded Nineveh,' we might infer that Nineveh and its neighbouring towns had no existence before the days when Babylonian emigrants settled in the territory of the city of Assur, and superseded its older inhabitants. However this may be, we know from the cuneiform monuments that the rise of Assyria did not take place until the Babylonian monarchy was already growing old. The country afterwards known as Assyria had been comprised in Gutium or Kurdistan, a name which has been identified, with great probability, by Sir H. Rawlinson, with the Goyyim or 'nations' of Genesis xiv. over which Tidal was king. There seems to have been a time when the rulers of Assur were mere governors appointed by the Babylonian monarchs; at all events, the earliest of whom we know do not give themselves the title of king, but use a word which signifies 'viceroy' in the Chaldean inscriptions.

These viceroys, however, managed eventually to shake off the yoke of their Babylonian masters, and one of them, Bel-kapkapi by name, established an independent kingdom at Assur in the 17th or 16th century before our era. His kingdom extended on both sides of the Tigris, and doubtless included the country north of the Greater Zab, where Nineveh was situated. The exact frontiers of Assyria, however, were never accurately fixed. They varied with the military power and conquests of its monarchs. Sometimes portions of the plateau of Mesopotamia on the west were comprehended within it, as well as the country through which the Tigris flowed, as far south as the borders of Babylonia, and as far north as the Kurdish mountains. At other times Assyria was confined to the narrow space within which its great cities stood.

The inhabitants of Assyria belonged to the Semitic stock, that is to say, they were allied in blood and language to the Hebrews, the Aramæans, and the Arabs. The older population had been either expelled or destroyed. The Assyrians thus differed from the Babylonians, who were a mixed race, partly Semitic and partly non-Semitic. The non-Semitic element is generally termed Accadian ; it spoke agglutinative dialects, and was the original possessor of the plain of Chaldæa. The Accadians invented the cuneiform system of writing, founded the chief cities and civilisation of Babylonia, and erected the earliest Babylonian monuments with which we are acquainted. It was only gradually that they yielded to the advance of the Semites ; in fact, the final triumph of the Semites in Babylonia was only effected by their amalgamation with the old population of the country, and their complete acceptance of Accadian culture. The Accadian language lingered long, and when it died out was preserved as a learned language, like Latin in our own day, which every educated Babylonian was expected to know.

It was natural, therefore, that the pure-blooded

Semites of Assyria and the mixed population of Babylonia should differ from one another in many respects.
The Babylonians were agriculturists, fond of literature
and peaceful pursuits. The Assyrians, on the contrary,
have been appropriately termed the Romans of the
East: they were a military people, caring for little else
save war and trade. Their literature, like their culture
and art, was borrowed from Babylonia, and they never
took kindly to it. Even under the magnificent patron-
age of Assur-bani-pal, Assyrian literature was an
exotic. It was cultivated only by the few; whereas in
Babylonia the greater part of the population seems to
have been able to read and write. If the Assyrian was
less luxurious than his Babylonian neighbour, he was
also less humane. Indeed, the Assyrian annals glory in
the record of a ferocity at which we stand aghast. On
the other hand, the Assyrian was not so superstitious as
the Babylonian, though he ascribed his successes to the
favour of Assur, and impaled the inhabitants of conquered towns or burnt them alive because they did not
believe in his national deity. He was, as Nahum
declared, the lion which 'did tear in pieces enough for
his whelps, and strangled for his lionesses, and filled
his holes with prey, and his dens with ravin.'

Assyria was so wholly a military power, that the
destruction of Nineveh not only destroyed the Assyrian
Empire but blotted out the Assyrian nation itself.
When 'the gates of the rivers' of Nineveh—the Tigris
and Khusur—were opened, and 'the palace dissolved,'

Assyria ceased to exist.  In the Sassanian period the
mounds which covered the ruins of the old city were for
a short time occupied by the houses of a village, but
these, too, disappeared after a while, and the very site
of Nineveh remained for centuries unknown.  Rich, in
1818, conjectured that the mounds of Kouyunjik, opposite the modern town of Mosul, concealed its ruins
beneath them, but it was not until the excavations of
the Frenchman Botta, in 1842, and the Englishman
Layard, in 1845, that the remains first of Dur-Sargon,
and then of Nineveh itself, were revealed to the eyes of
a wondering world.  The capital of the Assyrian Empire
was recovered, and with it the sculptured monuments of
its kings, and the relics of its clay-inscribed library.
The discovery came at an opportune moment.  The
cuneiform inscriptions of Persia had at last yielded up
their secrets to the patient sagacity of European
scholars, and had furnished the key to other inscriptions,
—also in cuneiform characters, but of a wholly different
kind, and expressing a wholly different language—which
now proved to be the long-lost records of the Assyrian
people.  Little by little the records were deciphered ;
fresh expeditions to the buried cities of Assyria and
Babylonia returned to Europe with fresh spoils, and it
is now possible to describe the history and even the
daily life and thoughts of a people who but half a
century ago were but a mere name.  The following
pages are intended to give a picture of that history and
life.

# CHAPTER II.

## ASSYRIAN HISTORY.

ASSYRIAN history, as we have seen, begins with the *patesis* or viceroys of the city of Assur. We know little about them except their names; contemporaneous annals do not commence until Assyria has ceased to be the dependency of a foreign power, and has become an independent kingdom. It was in the 17th or 16th century before the Christian era that Bel-kapkapi first gave himself the title of king. For two or three centuries afterwards our chief information about the monarchy he founded is derived from the relations, sometimes hostile and sometimes peaceable, which his successors had with Babylonia. One of them, however, Rimmon-nirari I by name (about B C. 1320), has left us an inscription in which he recounts the wars he waged against the Babylonians, the Kurds, the Aramæans, and the Shuites, nomad tribes who extended along the western bank of the Euphrates. It was his son, Shalmaneser I, to whom the foundation of Calah is ascribed. For six generations his descendants followed one another on the throne; then came Tiglath-Pileser I, who may be regarded as

the founder of the first Assyrian Empire. He carried his
arms as far as Cilicia and Malatiyeh on the west, and
the wild tribes of Kurdistan on the east; he overthrew
the Moschi or Meshech, defeated the Hittites and their
Colchian allies, and erected a memorial of his conquests
at the sources of the Tigris. The Hittite city of Pethor,
at the junction of the Euphrates and Sajur, was gar-
risoned with Assyrian soldiers, and at Arvad the Assyrian monarch symbolised his subjection of the Mediterranean by embarking in a ship and killing a dolphin
in the sea. In Nineveh he established a botanical
garden, which he filled with the strange trees he had
brought back with him from his campaigns. In B.C. 1130
he marched into Babylonia, and, after a momentary
repulse at the hands of the Babylonian king, defeated
his antagonists on the banks of the Lower Zab. Babylonia was ravaged, and Babylon itself was captured.

With the death of Tiglath-Pileser I, Assyrian history
becomes for awhile obscure. The sceptre fell into feeble
hands, and the distant conquests of the empire were
lost. It was during this period of abeyance that the
kingdom of David and Solomon arose in the west. The
Assyrian power did not revive until the reign of Assur-
dân II, whose son, Rimmon-nirari II (B.C. 911—889),
and great-grandson, Assur-natsir-pal (B.C. 883—858), led
their desolating armies through Western Asia, and
made the name of Assyria once more terrible to the
nations around them. Assur-natsir-pal was at once
one of the most ferocious and most energetic of the

Assyrian kings. His track was marked by impalements, by pyramids of human heads, and by other barbarities too horrible to be described. But his campaigns reached further than those of Tiglath-Pileser had done. Armenia, Mesopotamia, and Kurdistan, were overrun again and again; the Babylonians were forced to sue for peace; Sangara, the Hittite king of Carchemish, paid tribute, and the rich cities of Phœnicia poured their offerings into the treasury of Nineveh. The armies of Assyria penetrated even to Nizir, where the ark of the Chaldæan Noah was believed to have rested on the peak of Rowandiz. In Assyria itself the cities were embellished with the spoils of foreign conquest ; splendid palaces were erected, and Calah, which had fallen into decay, was restored. A library was erected there, and it became the favourite residence of Assur-natsir-pal.

He was succeeded by his son Shalmaneser II, so named, perhaps, after the original founder of Calah. Shalmaneser's military successes exceeded even those of his father, and his long reign of thirty-five years marks the climax of the first Assyrian Empire. His annals are chiefly to be found engraved on three monuments now in the British Museum. One of these is a monolith from Kurkh, a place about twenty miles from Diarbekr. The full-length figure of Shalmaneser is sculptured upon it, and the surface of the stone is covered with the inscription. Another monument is a small 'obelisk' of polished black stone, the upper part of which is shaped like three ascending steps. Inscriptions run

round its four sides, as well as small bas-reliefs repre
senting the tribute offered to 'the great king' by
foreign states. Among the tribute-bearers are the
Israelitish subjects of 'Jehu, son of Omri.' The third
monument is one which was discovered in 1878 at
Balawât, about nine miles from Nimrûd or Calah. It
consists of the bronze framework of two colossal doors,
of rectangular shape, twenty-two feet high and twenty-
six feet broad. The doors opened into a temple, and
were made of wood, to which the bronze was fastened
by means of nails. The bronze was cut into bands,
which ran in a horizontal direction across the doors, and
were each divided into two lines of embossed reliefs.
These reliefs were hammered out, and not cast, and the
rudeness of their execution proves that they were the
work of native artists, and not of the Phœnician settlers
in Nineveh, of whose skill in such work we have several
specimens. Short texts are added to explain the reliefs,
so that the various campaigns and cities represented in
them can all be identified. Among the cities is the
Hittite capital Carchemish, and the warriors of Armenia
are depicted in a costume strikingly similar to that of
the ancient Greeks.

Shalmaneser's first campaign was against the restless
tribes of Kurdistan. He then turned northward, and
fell upon the Armenian king of Van and the Mannâ or
Minni (see Jer. li. 27), who inhabited the country between
the mountains of Kotûr and Lake Urumiyeh. The
Hittites of Carchemish, with their allies from Cilicia and

other neighbouring districts, were next compelled to sue
for peace, and the acquisition of Pethor, which had been
lost after Tiglath-Pileser's death, again gave the Assyrians the command of the ford over the Euphrates.
The result of this was, that in B.C. 854 Shalmaneser
came into conflict with the kingdom of Hamath. The
common danger had roused Hadadezer of Damascus,
called Benhaded II in the Bible, to make common cause
with Hamath, and a confederacy was formed to resist
the Assyrian advance. Among the confederates 'Ahab
of Israel' is mentioned as furnishing the allies with
2,000 chari ts and 10,000 infantry. But the confederacy
was shattered at Karkar or Aroer, although Shalmaneser
had himself suffered too severely to be able to follow up
his victory. For a time, therefore, Syria remained unmolested, and the Assyrian king turned his attention to
Babylonia, which he reduced to a state of vassalage,
under the pretext of assisting the Babylonian sovereign
against his rebel brother.

Twelve years, however, after the battle of Karkar,
Shalmaneser was once more in the west. Hadadezer
had been succeeded by Hazael on the throne of Damascus, and it was against him that the full flood of Assyrian
power was turned. For some time he managed to stem
it, but in B.C. 841 he suffered a crushing defeat on the
heights of Shenir (see Deut. iii. 9), and his camp, along
with 1,121 chariots and 470 carriages, fell into the hands
of the Assyrians, who proceeded to besiege him in his
capital, Damascus The siege, however, was soon raised,

and Shalmaneser contented himself with ravaging the
Hauran and marching to Beyrout, where his image was
carved on the rocky promontory of Baal-rosh, at the
mouth of the Nahr el-Kelb.   It was while he was in
this neighbourhood that the ambassadors of Jehu arrived
with offers of tribute and submission.   The tribute, we
are told, consisted of 'silver, gold, a golden bowl, vessels
of gold, goblets of gold, pitchers of gold, a sceptre for
the king's hand and spear-handles,' and Jehu is errone-
ously entitled 'the son of Omri.'

After the defeat of Hazael Shalmaneser's expeditions
were only to distant regions like Phœnicia, Kappadokia,
and Armenia, for .the sake of exacting tribute.   No
further attempt was made at permanent conquest, and
after B.C. 834 the old king ceased to lead his armies in
person, the tartan or commander-in-chief taking his
place.   Not long afterwards a revolt broke out headed
by his eldest son, who seems to have thought that he
would have little difficulty in wresting the sceptre from
the hands of the enfeebled king.   Twenty-seven cities,
including Nineveh and Assur, joined the revolt, which
was, however, finally put down by the energy and
military capacity of Shalmaneser's second son Samas-
Rimmon, who succeeded him soon afterwards (B.C.
823—810).   On his death he was followed by his son
Rimmon-nirari III (810—781), who compelled Mariha
of Damascus to pay him tribute, as well as the
Phœnicians, Israelites, Edomites, and Philistines.   But
the vigour of the dynasty was beginning to fail.   A few

short reigns followed that of Rimmon-nirari, during which the first Assyrian Empire melted away. A formidable power arose in Armenia, the Assyrian armies were driven to the frontiers of their own country, and disaffection began to prevail in Assyria itself. At length, on the 15th of June, B.C. 763, an eclipse of the sun took place, and the city of Assur rose in revolt. The revolt lasted three years, and before it could be crushed the outlying provinces were lost. When Assur-nirari, the last of his line, ascended the throne in BC. 753, the empire was already gone, and the Assyrian cities themselves were surging with discontent. Ten years later the final blow was struck; the army declared itself against their monarch, and he and his dynasty fell together. On the 30th of Iyyar of the year B.C. 745, a military adventurer, Pul, seized the vacant crown, and assumed the venerable name of Tiglath-Pileser.

If we may believe Greek tradition, Tiglath-Pileser II began life as a gardener. Whatever might have been his origin, however, he proved to be a capable ruler, a good general, and a far-sighted administrator. He was the founder of the second Assyrian Empire, which differed essentially from the first. The first empire was at best a loosely-connected military organization; campaigns were made into distant countries for the sake of plunder and tribute, but little effort was made to retain the districts that had been conquered. Almost as soon as the Assyrian armies

C

were out of sight, the conquered nations shook off the
Assyrian yoke, and it was only in regions bordering on
Assyria that garrisons were left by the Assyrian king.
And whenever the Assyrian throne was occupied by
a weak or unwarlike prince, even these were soon
destroyed or forced to retreat homewards. Tiglath-
Pileser II, however, consolidated and organised the
conquests he made ; turbulent populations were deported
from their old homes, and the empire was divided
into satrapies or provinces, each of which paid a fixed
annual tribute to the imperial exchequer. For the
first time in history the principle of centralisation was
carried out on a large scale, and a bureaucracy began
to take the place of the old feudal nobility of Assyria.
But the second Assyrian Empire was not only an
organised and bureaucratic one, it was also commercial.
In carrying out his schemes of conquest Tiglath-
Pileser II was influenced by considerations of trade.
His chief object was to divert the commerce of Western
Asia into Assyrian hands. For this purpose every
effort was made to unite Babylonia with Assyria, to
overthrow the Hittites of Carchemish, who held the
trade of Asia Minor, as well as the high road to the
west, and to render Syria and the Phœnician cities
tributary. The policy inaugurated by Tiglath-Pileser
was successfully followed up by his successors.

Babylonia was the first to feel the results of the
change of dynasty at Nineveh. The northern part of it
was annexed to Assyria, and secured by a chain of

fortresses. Tiglath Pileser now attacked the Kurdish tribes, who were constantly harassing the eastern frontier of the kingdom, and chastised them severely, the Assyrian army forcing its way through the fastnesses of the Kurdish mountains into the very heart of Media. But Ararat, or Armenia, was still a dangerous neighbour, and accordingly Tiglath-Pileser's next campaign was against a confederacy of the nations of the north headed by Gurduris of Van. The confederacy was utterly defeated in Kommagênê, 72,950 prisoners falling into the hands of the Assyrians, and the way was opened into Syria. In B.C. 742 the siege of Arpad (now Tel Erfâd) began, and lasted two years. Its fall brought with it the submission of Northern Syria, and it was next the turn of Hamath to be attacked. Hamath was in alliance with Uzziah of Judah, and its king Eniel may have been of Jewish extraction. But the alliance availed nothing. Hamath was taken by storm, part of its population transported to Armenia, and their places taken by colonists from distant provinces of the empire, while nineteen of the districts belonging to it were annexed to Assyria. The kings of Syria now flocked to render homage and offer tribute to the Assyrian conqueror. Among them we read the names of Menahem of Samaria, Rezon of Syria, Hiram of Tyre, and Pisiris of Carchemish. This was the occasion when, as we learn from 2 Kings xv. 19, Menahem gave a thousand talents of silver to the Assyrian king Pul, the name under which Tiglath-Pileser continued to be known in Babylonia, and, as the Old Testament informs us, in Palestine also.

Three years later Ararat was again invaded. Van, the capital, was blockaded, and though it successfully resisted the Assyrians, the country was devastated far and near for a space of 450 miles. It was long before the Armenians recovered from the blow, and for the next century they ceased to be formidable to Assyria. Tiglath-Pileser's northern frontier was now secure, and he therefore gladly seized the opportunity of interfering in the affairs of the west which was offered him by Ahaz, the Jewish king. Ahaz, whom the Assyrian inscriptions call Jehoahaz, had been hard pressed by Rezon of Damascus and Pekah of Israel, who had combined to overthrow the Davidic dynasty and place a vassal prince, 'the son of Tabeal,' on the throne of Jerusalem. Ahaz in his extremity called in the aid of Tiglath-Pileser, offering him a heavy bribe and acknowledging his supremacy. Tiglath-Pileser accordingly marched into Syria; Rezon was utterly defeated in battle and then besieged in Damascus, to which he had escaped. Damascus was closely invested; the trees in its neighbourhood were cut down; the districts dependent on it were ravaged, and forces were despatched to punish the Israelites, Ammonites, Moabites, and Philistines, who had been the allies of Rezon, Gilead and Abel-beth-maachah being burnt, and the tribes beyond the Jordan carried into captivity. The Philistine cities were compelled to open their gates; the king of

Ashkelon committed suicide in order not to fall into the hands of the enemy, and Khanun of Gaza fled to Egypt. At last in B.C. 732, after a siege of two years, Damascus was forced by famine to surrender. Rezon was slain, Damascus given over to plunder and ruin, and its inhabitants transported to Kir. Syria became an Assyrian province, and all its princes were summoned to do homage to the conqueror, while Tyre was fined 150 talents of gold, or about £400,000. Among the princes who attended the levée or 'durbar' was Ahaz, and it was while he was attending it that he saw the altar of which he sent a pattern to Urijah the priest (2 Kings xvi. 10).

All that now remained for Tiglath-Pileser to do was to reduce Babylonia as he had reduced Syria. In B.C. 731, accordingly, he marched again into Chaldæa. Ukin-ziru, the Babylonian king, was slain, Babylon and other great cities were taken, and in B.C. 729, under his original name of Pul, Tiglath-Pileser assumed the title of ' king of Sumer (Shinar) and Accad.'

He lived only two years after this, and died in B.C. 727, when the crown was seized by Elulæos of Tinu, who took the name of Shalmaneser IV. Shalmaneser's short reign was signalised by an unsuccessful attempt to capture Tyre, and by the beginning of a war against the kingdom of Israel. But the siege of Samaria was hardly commenced when Shalmaneser died, or was murdered, in B.C. 722, and was succeeded by another usurper who assumed the name of Sargon, one of the most famous of the early Babylonian kings. Sargon in his inscriptions claims royal descent, but the claim was probably without foundation. He proved to be an able general, though his inscriptions show that he continued to the last to be a rough but energetic soldier who had perhaps risen from the ranks.

Two years after his accession (B.C. 720) Samaria was taken and placed under an Assyrian governor, 27,280 of its leading inhabitants being carried captive to Gozan and Media. But Sargon soon found that the task of cementing and completing the empire founded by Tiglath-Pileser was by no means an easy one. Babylonia had broken away from Assyria on the news of Shalmaneser's death, and had submitted itself to Merodach-Baladan the hereditary chieftain of Beth-Yagina in the marshes on the coast of the Persian Gulf. The southern portion of Sargons dominions was threatened by the ancient and powerful kingdom of Elam; the Kurdish tribes on the east renewed their depredations; while the Hittite kingdom of Carchemish still remained unsubdued, and the Syrian conquests could with difficulty be retained. In fact, a new enemy appeared in this part of the empire in the shape of Egypt.

Sargon's first act, therefore, was to drive the Elamites back to their own country with considerable loss. He was then recalled to the west by the revolt of Hamath, where Yahu-bihdi, or Ilu-bihdi, whose name perhaps indicates his Jewish parentage, had proclaimed himself

king, and persuaded Arpad, Damascus, Samaria, and
other cities to follow his standard. But the revolt was
of short duration. Hamath was burnt, 4,300 Assyrians
being sent to occupy its ruins, and Yahu-bihdi was
flayed alive. Sargon next marched along the sea-coast
to the cities of the Philistines. There the Egyptian
army was routed at Raphia, and its ally, Khanun of
Gaza, taken captive.

In B.C. 717 all was ready for dealing the final blow at
the Hittite power in Northern Syria. The rich trading
city of Carchemish was stormed, its last king, Pisiris,
fell into the hands of the Assyrians, and his Moschian
allies were forced to retreat to the north. The plunder
of Carchemish brought eleven talents and thirty manehs
of gold and 2,100 talents of silver into the treasury of
Calah. It was henceforth placed under an Assyrian
satrap, who thus held in his hands the key of the high
road and the caravan trade between Eastern and Western
Asia.

But Sargon was not allowed to retain possession of
Carchemish without a struggle. Its Hittite inhabitants
found avengers in 'the allied populations of the north, in
Meshech and Tubal, in Ararat and Minni. The struggle
lasted for six years, but in the end Sargon prevailed.
Van submitted, its king Ursa, the leader of the coalition
against Assyria, committed suicide, Cilicia and the
Tibareni or Tubal were placed under an Assyrian
governor, and the city of Malatiyeh was razed to the
ground. In B.C. 711, Sargon was at length free to

turn his attention to the west. Here affairs wore a threatening aspect. Merodach-Baladan, foreseeing that his own turn would come as soon as Sargon had firmly established his power in Northern Syria, had despatched ambassadors to the Mediterranean states, urging them to combine with him against the common foe. We read in the Bible of the arrival of the Babylonian embassy in Jerusalem, and of the rebuke received by Hezekiah for his vainglory in displaying to the strangers the resources of his kingdom. In spite of Isaiah's warning, Hezekiah listened to the persuasions of the Babylonian envoys, and encouraged by the promise of Egyptian support along with Phœnicia, Moab, Edom, and the Philistines, determined to defy the Assyrian king.

But before the confederates were ready to act in concert Sargon descended upon Palestine. Phœnicia and Judah were overrun, Jerusalem was captured, and Ashdod burnt, while the Egyptians made no attempt to help their friends. This siege of Ashdod is the only occasion on which the name of Sargon occurs in the Bible (Isaiah xx. 1). As soon as all source of danger was removed in the west Sargon hurled his forces against Babylonia. Merodach-Baladan had made every preparation to meet the coming attack, and the Elamite king had engaged to help him. But the Elamites were again compelled to fly before the warriors of Assyria, and Sargon entered Babylon in triumph (B.C. 710). The following year he pursued Merodach-Baladan to his ancestral stronghold in the marshes ; Beth-Yagina was taken by storm, and its unfortunate defenders were sent in chains to Nineveh. Sargon was now at the height of his power. His empire was a compact and consolidated whole, reaching from the Mediterranean on the west to the mountains of Elam on the east, and his solemn coronation at Babylon gave a title to his claim to be the legitimate successor of the ancient Sargon of Accad. The old kingdoms of Elam and Egypt alone remained to threaten the newly-founded empire, which received the voluntary homage of the smaller states that lay immediately beyond it. Thus the sacred island of Dilvun in the Persian Gulf submitted itself to the terrible conqueror, and the Phœnicians of Kition or Chittim in Cyprus erected a monumental record of his supremacy.

Sargon's end was consonant with his whole career. He was murdered by his soldiers in his new city of Dur-Sargon or Khorsabad, on the 12th of Ab or July, B.C. 705, and was succeeded by his son Sennacherib. If we may judge from Sennacherib's name, which means 'the Moon-god has increased the brothers,' he would not have been Sargon's eldest son. In any case he had been brought up in the purple, and displayed none of the rugged virtues of his father. He was weak, boastful, and cruel, and preserved his empire only by the help of the veterans and generals whom Sargon had trained.

Merodach-Baladan had escaped from captivity, and two years after the death of Sargon had once more possessed himself of Babylon. But a battle at Kis drove him from the country nine months subsequently, and Sennacherib was able to turn his attention to affairs in the west. In B C. 701, he marched into Phœnicia and Palestine, where Hezekiah of Judah and some of the neighbouring kings had refused their tribute. Tirhakah, the Ethiopian king of Egypt, had promised support to the rebellious states, and Padi, the king of Ekron, who remained faithful to the Assyrians, was carried in chains to Jerusalem. The Assyrian army fell first upon Phœnicia. Great and Little Sidon, Sarepta, Acre, and other towns, surrendered, Elulæos, the Sidonian monarch, fled to Cyprus, and the kings of Arvad and Gebal offered homage. Metinti of Ashdod, Pedael of Ammon, Chemosh-nadab of Moab, and Melech-ram of Edom, also submitted. Then, says Sennacherib: 'Zedekiah, king of Ashkelon, who had not submitted to my yoke, himself, the gods of the house of his fathers, his wife, his sons, his daughters, and his brothers, the seed of the house of his fathers, I removed, and I sent him to Syria. I set over the men of Ashkelon Sarludari, the son of Rukipti, their former king, and I imposed upon him the payment of tribute, and the homage due to my majesty, and he became a vassal. In the course of my campaign I approached and captured Beth-Dagon, Joppa, Bene-berak, and Azur, the cities of Zedekiah, which did not submit at once to my yoke, and I carried away their spoil. The priests, the chief men, and the common people of Ekron who had thrown into chains their king Padi because he was faithful to his oaths to Assyria, and had given him up to Hezekiah, the Jew, who imprisoned him like an enemy in a dark dungeon, feared in their hearts. The king of Egypt, the bowmen, the chariots, and the horses of the king of Ethiopia, had gathered together innumerable forces, and gone to their assistance. In sight of the town of Eltekeh was their order of battle drawn up; they called their troops (to the battle). Trusting in Assur, my lord, I fought with them and overthrew them. My hands took the captains of the chariots, and the sons of the king of Egypt, as well as the captains of the chariots of the king of Ethiopia, alive in the midst of the battle. I approached and captured the towns of Eltekeh and Timnath, and I carried away their spoil. I marched against the city of Ekron, and put to death the priests and the chief men who had committed the sin (of rebellion), and I hung up their bodies on stakes all round the city. The citizens who had done wrong and wickedness I counted as a spoil; as for the rest of them who had done no sin or crime, in whom no fault was found, I proclaimed a free pardon. I had Padi, their king, brought out from the midst of Jerusalem, and I seated him on the throne of royalty over them, and I laid upon him the tribute due to my majesty. But as for Hezekiah of Judah, who had not submitted to my yoke, forty-six of his strong cities, together with innumerable fortresses and small towns which depended on them, by overthrowing the walls and open attack, by battle engines and battering-rams, I besieged, I captured,

I brought out from the midst of them and counted as a
spoil 200,150 persons, great and small, male and female,
horses, mules, asses, camels, oxen and sheep without
number.   Hezekiah himself I shut up like a bird in a
cage in Jerusalem, his royal city.   I built a line of forts
against him, and I kept back his heel from going forth
out of the great gate of his city.   I cut off his cities that
I had spoiled from the midst of his land, and gave them
to Metinti, king of Ashdod, Padi, king of Ekron, and
Zil-baal, king of Gaza, and I made his country small.   In
addition to their former tribute and yearly gifts, I added
other tribute, and the homage due to my majesty, and
I laid it upon them.   The fear of the greatness of my
majesty overwhelmed him, even Hezekiah, and he sent
after me to Nineveh, my royal city, by way of gift and
tribute, the Arabs and his body-guard whom he had
brought for the defence of Jerusalem, his royal city, and
had furnished with pay, along with thirty talents of
gold, 800 talents of pure silver, carbuncles and other
precious stones, a couch of ivory, thrones of ivory, an
elephant's hide, an elephant's tusk, rare woods of various
names, a vast treasure, as well as the eunuchs of his
palace, dancing-men and dancing-women ; and he sent
his ambassador to offer homage.'

In this account of his campaign Sennacherib discreetly
says nothing about the disaster which befell his army
in front of Jerusalem, and which obliged him to return
ignominiously to Assyria without attempting to capture
Jerusalem, and to deal with Hezekiah as it was his

custom to deal with other rebellious kings. The tribute offered by Hezekiah at Lachish, when he vainly tried to buy off the threatened Assyrian attack, is represented as having been the final result of a successful campaign. There is, however, no exaggeration in the amount of silver Sennacherib claims to have received, since 800 talents of silver are equivalent to the 500 talents stated by the Bible to have been given, when reckoned according to the standard of value in use at the time in Nineveh.

Sennacherib never recovered from the blow he had suffered in Judah. He made no more expeditions against Palestine, and during the rest of his reign Judah remained unmolested. Babylonia, moreover, gave him constant trouble. In the year after his campaign in the west (B.C. 700) a Chaldean, named Nergal-yusezib, stirred up a revolt which Sennacherib had some difficulty in suppressing. Two years later he appointed his eldest son, Assur-nadin-sumi, viceroy of Babylon. In B.C. 694, he determined to attack the followers of Merodach-Baladan in their last retreat at the mouth of the Eulæus, where land had been given to them by the Elamite king after their expulsion from Babylonia. Ships were built and manned by Phœnicians in the Persian Gulf, by means of which the settlements of the Chaldean refugees were burnt and destroyed. Meanwhile, however, Babylonia itself was invaded by the Elamites; the Assyrian viceroy was carried into captivity, and Nergal-yusezib placed on the throne of the country. He defeated the Assyrian forces in a

battle near Nipur, but died soon afterwards, and was
followed by Musezib-Merodach, who like his pre-
decessor is called Suzub in Sennacherib's inscriptions.
He defied the Assyrian power for nearly four years.
But in B.C. 690 the combined Babylonian and Elamite
army was overthrown in the decisive battle of Khalule,
and before another year was past Sennacherib had
captured Babylon, and given it up to fire and sword.
Its inhabitants were sold into slavery, and the waters
of the Araxes canal allowed to flow over its ruins.
Sennacherib now assumed the title of king of Babylonia,
but with the exception of a campaign into the Cilician
mountains he seems to have undertaken no more
military expeditions. The latter years of his life were
passed in constructing canals and aqueducts, in
embanking the Tigris, and in rebuilding the palace of
Nineveh on a new and sumptuous scale. On the
20th of Tebet, or December, B.C. 681, he was murdered
by his two elder sons, Adrammelech and Nergal-shareze,
who were jealous of the favour shown to their younger
brother, Esar-haddon.

Esar-haddon was at the time conducting a campaign
against Erimenas, king of Armenia, to whom his
insurgent brothers naturally fled. Between seven and
eight weeks after the murder of the old king, a battle
was fought near Malatiyeh, in Kappadokia, between
the veterans of Esar-haddon and the forces under his
brothers and Erimenas, which ended in the complete
defeat of the latter. Esar-haddon was proclaimed king,

and the event proved that a wiser choice could not have been made.

His military genius was of the first order, but it was equalled by his political tact. He was the only king of Assyria who endeavoured to conciliate the nations he had conquered. Under him the fabric of the Second Empire was completed by the conquest of Egypt. In the first year of his reign he rebuilt Babylon, giving it back its captured deities, its plunder, and its people. Henceforth Babylon became the second capital of the empire, the court residing alternately there and at Nineveh. It was while Esar haddon was holding his winter court at Babylon that Manasseh, of Judah, was brought to him as prisoner.[1]

The trade of Phœnicia was diverted into Assyrian hands by the destruction of Sidon. The caravan-road from east to west was at the same time rendered secure by an expedition into the heart of Northern Arabia. Here Esar-haddon penetrated as far as the lands of Huz and Buz, 280 miles of the march being through a waterless desert. The feat has never been excelled, and the terror it inspired among the Bedouin tribes was not forgotten for many years. The northern frontiers of the kingdom were also made safe by the defeat of Teispes, the Kimmerian, who was driven westward with his hordes into Asia Minor. In the east the Assyrian monarch was bold enough to occupy and work the copper-mines on the distant borders of Media, the very

[1] 2 Chr. xxxiii. 11.

name of which had scarcely been heard of before. Westward, the kings of Cyprus paid homage to the great conqueror, and among the princes who sent materials for his palace at Nineveh were Cyprian rulers with Greek names.

But the principal achievement of Esar-haddon's reign was his conquest of the ancient monarchy of Egypt. In B.C. 675 the Assyrian army started for the banks of the Nile. Four years later Memphis was taken on the 22nd of Tammuz, or June, and Tirhakah, the Egyptian king, compelled to fly first to Thebes, and then into Ethiopia. Egypt was divided into twenty satrapies, governed partly by Assyrians, partly by native princes, whose conduct was watched by Assyrian garrisons. On his return to Assyria Esar-haddon associated Assur-bani pal, the eldest of his four sons, in the government on the 12th of Iyyar, or April, B.C. 669, and died two years afterwards (on the 12th of Marchesvan, or October), when again on his way to Egypt. Assur-bani-pal, the Sardanapalos of the Greeks, succeeded to the empire, his brother, Samas-sum-yukin, being entrusted with the government of Babylonia.

Assur-bani-pal is probably the 'great and noble' Asnapper of Ezra iv. 10. He was luxurious, ambitious, and cruel, but a munificent patron of literature. The libraries of Babylonia were ransacked for ancient texts, and scribes were kept busily employed at Nineveh in inscribing new editions of older works. But unlike his fathers, Assur-bani-pal refused to face the hardships of

ASSUR-BANI-PAL AND HIS QUEEN.

*From the original in the British Museum.*

D

a campaign. His armies were led by generals, who were required to send despatches from time to time to the king. It was evident that a purely military empire, like that of Assyria, could not last long, when its ruler had himself ceased to take an active part in military affairs. At first the veterans of his father preserved and even extended the empire of Assur-bani-pal; but before his death it was shattered irretrievably. It is characteristic of Assur-bani-pal that his lion-hunts were mere *battues*, in which tame animals were released from cages and lashed to make them run; in curious contrast to the lion hunts in the open field in which his warlike predecessors had delighted.

His first occupation was to crush a revolt in Egypt. Tirhakah was once more driven out of the country, and Thebes, called Ni in the Assyrian texts, and No-Amon, or 'No of the god Amun' in Scripture, was plundered and destroyed. Its temples were hewed in pieces, and two of its obelisks, weighing 70 tons in all, were carried as trophies to Nineveh. It is to this destruction of the old capital of the Pharaohs that Nahum refers in his prophecy (iii. 8).

Meanwhile Tyre had been besieged and forced to surrender, and Cilicia had paid homage to the Assyrian king. Gog, or Gyges, of Lydia, too, voluntarily sent him tribute, including two Kimmerian chieftains whom the Lydian sovereign had captured in battle. When the Lydian ambassadors arrived in Nineveh they found no one who could understand their language; in fact, the very name of Lydia had been unknown to the Assyrians before.

The Assyrian Empire had now reached its widest limits. Elam had fallen after a long and arduous struggle. Shushan, its capital, was razed to the ground, and the three last Elamite kings were bound to the yoke of Assur-bani-pal's chariot, and made to drag their conqueror through the streets of Nineveh. The Kedarites and other nomad tribes of Northern Arabia were also chastised, the land of the Minni was overrun, and the Armenians of Van begged for an alliance with the Assyrian king.

But while at the very height of his prosperity, the empire was fast slipping away from under Assur-bani-pal's feet. In B C. 652 a rebellion broke out headed by his brother, the Babylonian viceroy, which shook it to the foundations. Babylonia, Egypt, Palestine, and Arabia made common cause against the oppressor. Lydia sent Karian and Ionic mercenaries to Psammetikhos of Sais, with whose help he succeeded in overthrowing his brother satraps, and in delivering Egypt from the Assyrian yoke. The revolt in Babylonia took long to quell, and for a time the safety of Assur-bani-pal himself was imperilled. At last in 647 Babylon and Cuthah were reduced by famine, and Samas-sum-yukin burnt himself to death in his palace. Fire and sword were carried through Elam, and the last of its monarchs became an outlawed fugitive.

When Assyria finally emerged from the deadly struggle, Egypt was lost to it for ever, and Babylonia was but half subdued. The latter province was placed under the government of Kandalanu, who ruled over it for twenty-two years, more like an independent sovereign than a viceroy. His successor, Nabopolassar, the father of Nebuchadnezzar, threw off all semblance of submission to Nineveh, and prepared the way for the empire of his son. But meanwhile the once proud kingdom of Assyria had been contending for bare existence. Assur-bani-pal's son, Assur-etil-ilani, rebuilt with diminished splendour the palace of Calah, which seems to have been burnt by some victorious enemy; and when the last Assyrian king, Esar-haddon II, called Sarakos by the Greeks, mounted the throne, he found himself surrounded on all sides by threatening foes. Kaztarit or Kyaxares, Mamitarsu the Median, the Kimmerians, the Minni, and the people of Sepharad leagued themselves together against the devoted city of Nineveh. The frontier towns fell first, and though Esar-haddon in his despair proclaimed public fasts and prayers to the gods, nothing could ward off the doom pronounced by God's prophets against Nineveh so long before. Nineveh was besieged, captured, and utterly destroyed; and the second Assyrian Empire perished more hopelessly and completely than the first. All that survived was the old capital of the country, Assur, whose former inhabitants were allowed to return to it by Cyrus at the time when the Jewish exiles also were released from their captivity in Babylon.[1]

[1] The following are the significations of the different Assyrian royal names mentioned in this chapter :—

Rimmon-nirari, 'Rimmon (the Air-god) is my help.'

Shalmaneser (Sallimanu-esir, 'Sallimanu (Solomon, 'the god of peace directs.' The Babylonians changed the name to Sulman-asarid, 'Solomon is supreme.'

Tiglath-Pileser Tukult -pal-E-Sára), 'The servant of (the god Adar the son f E-'Sara the temple of legions).'

Assur-dân, 'Assur is strong '

Assur-natsir-pal, 'Assur is protector of the son.'

Samas-Rimmon, 'The Sun-god is also Rimmon (the Air-god .'

Sargon (Sarru-kunu), 'the constituted king.'

Sennacherib (Sinu-akhi-erba), 'The Moon-god increased the brethren.'

Esar-haddon (Assur akh-iddina), 'Assur gave a brother.'

Assur-bani-pal, 'Assur is creator of the son.'

Assur-etil-'lani, 'Assur is prince of the gods.'

# CHAPTER III.

## Assyrian Religion.

THE Assyrians derived the greater part of their deities and religious beliefs, like their literature and culture generally, from Babylonia. The Babylonian gods were the gods of Assyria also. Most of them were of Accadian or præ-Semitic origin, but the Semitic Babylonians, when they appropriated the civilisation of the Accadians, modified them in accordance with their own conceptions. The Accadians believed that every object and phenomenon of nature had its *Zi* or ' spirit,' some of them beneficent, others hostile to man, like the objects and phenomena they represented. Naturally, however, there were more malevolent than beneficent spirits in the universe, and there was scarcely an action which did not risk demoniac possession. Diseases were due to the malevolence of these spirits, and could be cured only by the use of certain charms and exorcisms. Exorcisms, in fact, gave those who employed them power over the spirits ; they could by means of them compel the evil spirit to retire, and the beneficent spirit to approach. The knowledge of such exorcisms was in the hands of the priests, so that priest and magician were almost synonymous terms.

Among the multitude of spirits feared by the
Accadians, there were some which had been raised
above the rest into the position of gods. Of these, Anu,
'the sky;' Mul-ge, 'the earth;' and Ea, 'the deep,'
were the most conspicuous. At their side stood the
'spirits' of the heavenly bodies—the Moon-god, the
Sun-god, the evening star, and the other planets. The
Moon-god ranked before the Sun-god, as might indeed
have been expected to be the case among a nation of
astronomers like the Chaldeans.

When the Semitic Babylonians adopted the deities of
their predecessors and teachers, Anu and his compeers
lost much of their elemental nature, while the Sun-god
Samas came to assume an important place. The religion
of the Babylonian Semites, in fact, was essentially solar;
the Sun-god was addressed as Bel or Baal, the supreme
'lord,' and adored under various forms. He appeared
to them, moreover, under two aspects, sometimes as the
kindly deity who gives life and light to all things,
sometimes as the scorching sun of summer who
demanded the sacrifice of the first-born to appease his
wrath. Sometimes, again, he was worshipped as the
young and beautiful Tammuz, slain by the boar's tusk
of winter; whose death was lamented at the autumnal
equinox, and who was invoked as *adoni* (*Adonis*) or
'master.'

Unlike the Accadians, who did not distinguish
gender, the Semites divided all nouns into masculines
and feminines. By the side of the god, consequently,

stood the goddess. She was, however, but a pale reflection of her male consort, created, so to speak, by the necessities of grammar. She had no independent attributes of her own ; Beltis, or Bilat, the wife of Bel, was nothing more than the feminine complement of the god. The Accadians had known of one great goddess, Istar, the evening star ; but Istar was an independent deity, with attributes as strongly and individually marked as those of the gods. Among the Semites, Istar became Ashtoreth, with the feminine suffix *th*, and though in Babylonia the old legends and traditions prevented her from losing altogether her primitive character, she tended more and more to pass into the mere reflection of some male deity. Just as the gods could be collectively spoken of as Baalim or 'lords,' all being regarded as so many different forms of the Sun-god, the goddesses also were termed Ashtaroth or ' Ashtoreths.'

We see, therefore, that in adopting the pantheon of Accad, the Semites made three important changes. The Sun-god was assigned a leading place in worship and belief ; female deities were introduced, who were, however, mere reflections of the gods ; while the inferior deities of the Accadians were classed among 'the 300 spirits of heaven' and 'the 600 spirits of earth,' only a few of the more prominent ones retaining their old position. These latter may be grouped as follows :—

At the head of the divine hierarchy still stood the old triad of Anu, Mul-ge, and Ea. Mul-ge's name, however,

was changed to Bel, but since Merodach was also known
as Bel, he fell more and more into the background,
especially after the rise of Babylon, of which city
Merodach was the patron deity.  At Nipur, now Niffer,
alone, he continued to be worshipped down into late
times.  His consort was Bilat, or Beltis, 'the great lady,'
who eventually came to be regarded as the wife of
Merodach rather than of 'the other Bel.'  Like Anu and
Ea, Bel was the offspring of Sar and Kisar, the upper
and lower firmaments.

Anu was the visible sky, but he also represented the
invisible heaven, which was supposed to extend above
the visible one, and to be the abode of the gods.  The
chief seat of his worship was Erech, where he was
regarded as the oldest of the gods, and the original
creator of the universe.  But elsewhere, also, he was
looked upon as the creator of the visible world, and the
father of the gods.  By his side, in the Semitic period,
stood the goddess Anat, whose attributes were derived
from his.  The worship of Anat spread from Babylonia
to the Canaanites, as is shown by the geographical
names Beth Anath, 'the temple of Anat' (Josh. xix. 38 ;
xv. 59), and Anathoth, the city of 'the goddesses Anat.'
It was even introduced into Egypt after the Asiatic
wars of the eighteenth dynasty.  In the præ-Semitic days
of Chaldea, a monotheistic school had flourished, which
resolved the various deities of the Accadian belief into
manifestations of the one supreme god, Anu ; and old
hymns exist in which reference is made to 'the one

god.' But this school never seems to have numbered many adherents, and it eventually died out. Its existence, however, reminds us of the fact that Abraham was born in ' Ur of the Chaldees.'

Ea originally represented the ocean-stream or 'great deep,' which was supposed to surround the earth like a serpent, and by which all rivers and springs were fed. He was symbolised by the snake, and was held to be the creator and benefactor of mankind. One of his most frequent titles is 'lord of wisdom,' and the chief seat of his worship was at Eridu, 'the holy city,' near which was the sacred grove or 'garden,' the centre of the world, where the tree of life and knowledge had its roots. It was Ea who had given to mankind not only life, but all the arts and appliances of culture also, and it was his help that the Babylonian invoked when in trouble. He was emphatically the god of healing, who had revealed medicines to mankind. As god of the great deep, he was often figured as a man with the tail of a fish, and in this form was known to the Greeks under the name of Oannes or ' Ea the fish.' Sometimes the skin of a fish was suspended behind his back. Oannes, it was said, had in early days ascended out of the Persian Gulf, and taught the first inhabitants of Babylonia letters, science, and art, besides writing a history of the origin of mankind and their different ways of life. His wife was Dav-kina, 'the lady of the earth,' who presided over the lower world.

Among the numerous offspring of Ea and Dav-kina,

Merodach held the foremost place. He was originally a form of the Sun-god, regarded under his beneficent aspect, and was believed to be ever engaged in combating the powers of evil, and in performing services for mankind. Hence he is addressed as 'the redeemer of mankind,' 'the restorer to life,' and the 'raiser from the dead,' and a considerable number of the religious hymns are dedicated to him. He was believed to be continually passing backwards and forwards between the earth and the heaven where Ea dwelt, informing Ea of the sufferings of men, and returning with Ea's directions how to relieve them. One of the bas-reliefs from Nineveh, now in the British Museum, represents him as pursuing with his curved sword or thunderbolt the demon Tiamat, the personification of chaos and anarchy, who is depicted with claws, tail, and horns. As we have already seen, he was commonly addressed as Bel or 'lord,' and so came gradually to supplant the older Bel or Mul ge. Among the planets his star was Jupiter. His wife was Zarpanit or Zirat-panitu, in whom some scholars have seen the Succoth-benoth of 2 Kings xvii. 30.

The children of Merodach and Zarpanit were Nebo, 'the prophet,' and his wife Tasmit, 'the hearer.' Nebo was the god of oratory and literature; it was he who 'enlightened the eyes' to understand written characters, while his wife 'enlarged the ears,' so that they could comprehend what was read. The origin of the cuneiform system of writing was ascribed to Nebo. To him was dedicated 'the temple of the Seven Lights of Heaven and Earth,' at Borsippa, the suburb of Babylon, which is now known to the Arabs as the Birs-i Nimrûd, and his worship was carried as far as Canaan, as we may gather from such names as the city of Nebo, in Judæa (Ezra ii. 29), and Mount Nebo, in Moab (Deut. xxxii. 49). In Accadian he had been called Dimsar, 'the tablet-writer,' and a temple was erected to him in the island of Bahrein, in the Persian Gulf, where he was worshipped under the name of Enzak. As a planetary deity, he was identified with Mercury. He was often adored under the name of Nusku, although Nusku had originally been a separate divinity, and the same, perhaps, as the Nisroch of the Bible (2 Kings xix. 37).

The companion of Merodach was Rimmon, or rather Ramman, 'the thunderer.' He represented the atmosphere, and was accordingly the god of rain and storm, who was armed with the lightning and the thunderbolt. Sometimes he was dreaded as 'the destroyer of crops,' 'the scatterer of the harvest;' at other times prayers were made to him as 'the lord of fecundity.' His worship extended into Syria, where Rimmon appears to have been the supreme deity of Damascus, and where he was also known under the name of Hadad or Dadda.

Two other elemental gods were Samas, the Sun-god, and Sin, the Moon-god. Samas was the son of Sin, in accordance with the astronomical view of the old Babylonians, which made the moon the measurer of time, and regarded the day as the offspring of night. Samas, however, like Saul or Savul, another deity of

whom mention is made in the inscriptions, was really
but a form of Merodach, though in historical times the
two divinities were separated from one another, and
received different cults. Samas, again, was originally
identical with Tammuz ; but when Tammuz came to
denote only the sun of spring and summer, while the
myth that associated him with Istar laid firm hold
of men's minds, Tammuz assumed separate attributes,
and an individual existence apart from Samas.

Sin, the Moon-god, was termed Agu or Acu by the
Accadians, and if the name of Mount Sinai was derived
from him, as is sometimes supposed, we should have
evidence that he was known and worshipped in Northern
Arabia. At all events he was one of the deities of
Southern Arabia. Sin was the patron-god of the city of
Ur, and it was to him that the Assyrian kings traced
the formation of their kingdom. One of the most famous
of his temples was in the ancient city of Harran, where
he was symbolised by an upright cone of stone. As the
emblem of the Sun-god was the solar orb, the emblem
of Sin was the crescent moon.

According to some of the legends of Babylonia, the
daughter of the Moon-god was the goddess Istar. Other
legends, however, placed Istar among the older gods,
and made her the daughter of Anu, the sky. In either
case she was at the outset the goddess of the evening
star, and when it was discovered that the evening and
morning stars were the same, of the morning star also.
As the evening star, she was known as Istar of Erech, as

the morning star, she was identified with Anunit or Anat, the goddess of Accad. At times she was also regarded as androgynous, both male and female.

Istar was the chief of the Accadian goddesses, and she retained her rank even among the Semites, who, as we have seen, looked upon the goddess as the mere consort and shadow of the god. But Istar continued to the last a separate and independent divinity. She presided over love and war, as well as over the chase. She was invoked as 'the queen of heaven,' 'the queen of all the gods,' and there was often a tendency to merge in her the other goddesses of the pantheon. Her principal temples were at Erech, Nineveh, and Arbela, but altars were erected to her in almost every place, and she was adored under as many forms and titles as she possessed shrines. Her name and worship spread through the Semitic world, in Southern Arabia, in Syria, in Moab, where she was identified with the Sun-god, Chemosh, and in Canaan, where she was called Ashtoreth, the Astarté of the Greeks. But the Greeks also knew her as Aphrodîtê, the goddess whom they had borrowed from the Phœnicians of Canaan, and we may discover her again in the Ephesian Artemis. The rites performed in her temples made Istar or Ashtoreth the darkest blot in Assyrian and Canaanitish religion, and excited the utmost horror and indignation of the prophets of God. When the moon came to be conceived as a female divinity, the pale reflection, as it were, of the sun, Istar, the evening star, became also the goddess of the moon.

Hence it is that 'the queen of heaven' (Jer. xliv. 17) passed into Astarté 'with crescent horns.'

One of the most popular of old Babylonian myths told how Istar had wedded the young and beautiful Sun-god, Tammuz, 'the only begotten,' and had descended into Hades in search of him when he had been slain by the boar's tusk of winter. A portion of a Babylonian poem has been preserved to us, which describes her passage through the seven gates of the underworld, where she left with the warden of each some one of her adornments, until at last she reached the seat of the infernal goddess Allat, stripped and bare. There she remained imprisoned until the gods, wearied of the long absence of the goddess of love, created a hound called 'the renewal of light,' who restored her to the upper world. The myth clearly refers to the waning and waxing of the monthly moon, and must therefore have originated when Istar had already become the goddess of the moon. The myth entered deeply into the religious belief of the worshippers of Istar. The Accadians called the month of August 'the month of the errand of Istar,' while June was termed 'the month of Tammuz' by the Semites. It was then that, as Milton writes, his

> 'annual wound in Lebanon allured
> The Syrian damsels to lament his fate
> In amorous ditties all a summer's day;
> While smooth Adonis from his native rock
> Ran purple to the sea, supposed with blood
> Of Tammuz yearly wounded.'

But it was not only in Assyria and Phœnicia that the death of Tammuz was lamented by the women year by year. The infection spread to Judah also, and even in Jerusalem, within the precincts of the temple itself, Ezekiel saw 'women weeping for Tammuz' (Ezek. viii. 14).

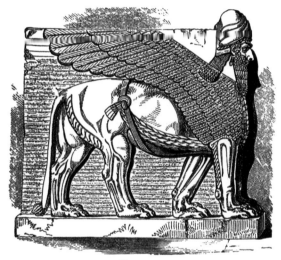

NERGAL.
*(From the original in the British Museum.)*

There are only two other Assyro-Babylonian deities who need be mentioned, Nergal and Adar. Nergal was the presiding deity of Cuthah and its vast necropolis.[1] He shared with Anu the privilege of superintending the regions of the dead, and he was also a god of hunting and war. His name, like those of Anu, Ea, and Istar,

[1] Confer 2 Kings xvii. 30.

E

was of Accadian origin.   Adar, the son of Beltis, was one
of those solar deities who were formed by worshipping
the Sun-god under some particular attribute.   The
reading of his name is, unfortunately, not certain, and
Adar is only its most probable pronunciation.   If it is
correct, Adar will be the deity meant in 2 Kings xvii.
31, where it is stated that the people of Sepharvaim, or
the two Sipparas, burnt their children in fire to Adrammelech and Anammelech, that is to say, to 'King Adar'
and 'King Anu.'

Such were the principal divinities of Babylonia and
Assyria.   But the Assyrians had another also, whom
they exalted above all the rest.   This was Assur, the
divine impersonation of the state and empire.   It was
Assur who, according to the Assyrian kings, led them to
victory, and the cruelties they practised on the conquered
were, they held, judgments exercised against those who
would not believe in him.   Assur, in the form of an
archer, is sometimes represented on the monuments in
the midst of the winged solar disk, and above the head
of the monarch, whom he protects from his enemies.

The Assyrian, however, was not so pious or superstitious as his Babylonian neighbour.   The Babylonian
lived in perpetual dread of the evil spirits which thronged
about him ; almost every moment had its religious
ceremony, almost every action its religious complement.
Not only had the State ritual to be attended to ; the
unceasing attacks of the demons could be warded off
only by magical incantations and the intervention of the

sorcerer-priest. But the Assyrians were too much occupied with wars and fighting to give all this heed to the requirements of religion. It is significant that, whereas in Babylonia we find the remains of scarcely any great buildings except temples, the great buildings of Assyria were the royal palaces. The libraries, which in Babylonia were stored in the temples, were deposited in Assyria in the palace of the king.

Nevertheless, the greater part of the religious system of Babylonia had been transported into Assyria. Along with the Babylonian deities had come the Babylonian scriptures. These were divided into two great collections or volumes. The first, and oldest, was a collection of exorcisms and magical texts, by the use of which, it was believed, the spirits of evil could be driven away, and the spirits of good induced to visit the reciter. When, however, certain independent deities began to emerge from among the multitudinous 'spirits' of the primitive Accadian creed, hymns were composed in their honour, and these hymns were eventually collected together, and, like the Rig-Veda of India, became a second sacred book. After the Accadians had been supplanted by the Semites, the Accadian language, in which the hymns were originally written, was provided with a Semitic translation ; but it was still considered necessary to recite the exact words of the original, since the words themselves were sacred, and any mistake in their pronunciation would invalidate the religious service in which they were employed. Some of the incantations embodied in the

E 2

collection of exorcisms must have been introduced into it subsequently to the compilation of the sacred hymns, since the latter are found inserted in them.   From this it would appear that the older collection continued to receive additions for a long while after the younger collection—that of the sacred hymns—had been put together and invested with a sacred character.   This could not have been till after the beginning of the Semitic period, since there are a few hymns which do not seem to have had any Accadian originals.   If we may compare the two collections with our own religious literature, we may say that the collection of hymns corresponded more to our Bible, that of exorcisms to our Prayer Book.

The Babylonians and Assyrians, however, possessed a liturgy which answered far better to our conception of what a Prayer Book should be.   This contained services for particular days and hours, together with rubrics for the direction of the priest.   Thus we are told that 'in the month Nisan, on the second day, two hours after nightfall, the priest [of Bel at Babylon] must come and take of the waters of the river, must enter into the presence of Bel, and change his dress; must put on a robe in the presence of Bel, and say this prayer: "O my lord who in his strength has no equal, O my lord, blessed sovereign, lord of the world, speeding the peace of the great gods, the lord who in his might destroys the strong, lord of kings, light of mankind, establisher of trust, O Bel, thy sceptre is Babylon, thy crown is

Borsippa, the wide heaven is the dwelling-place of thy liver. . . . O lord of the world, light of the spirits of heaven, utterer of blessings, who is there whose mouth murmurs not of thy righteousness, or speaks not of thy glory, and celebrates not thy dominion? O lord of the world, who dwellest in the temple of the sun, reject not the hands that are raised to thee; be merciful to thy city Babylon, to Beth-Saggil thy temple incline thy face, grant the prayers of thy people the sons of Babylon." '

Part of the liturgy consisted of prayers addressed to the various deities, and suited to various occasions. Here are examples of them: 'At dawn and in the night prayer should be made to the throne-bearer, and thus should it be said : "O throne-bearer, giver of prosperity, a prayer!" After that, let prayer be made to Nusku, and thus let it be said : "O Nusku, prince and king of the secrets of the great gods, a prayer!" After that, let prayer be made to Adar, and thus let it be said: "O Adar, mighty lord of the deep places of the springs, a prayer!" After that let prayer be made to Gula (Beltis), and thus let it be said : "O Gula, mother, begetter of the black headed race (of Accadians), a prayer!" After that, let prayer be made to Nin-lil, and thus let it be said : "O Nin-lil, great goddess, wife of the divine prince of sovereignty, a prayer!" After that, let prayer be made to Bel, and thus let it be said : "O lord supreme, establisher of law, a prayer!" The prayer (must be repeated) during the day at dawn, and in the night,

with face and mouth uplifted, during the middle watch.
Water must be poured out in libation day by day
. . . at dawn, on the beams of the palace.'

One of the most curious of these petitions is a prayer
after a bad dream, of which a fragment only has been
found. This reads as follows: 'May the lord set my
prayer at rest, (may he remove) my heavy (sin). May
the lord (grant) a return of favour. By day direct unto
death all that disquiets me. O my goddess, be gracious
unto me; when (wilt thou hear) my prayer? May they
pardon my sin, my wickedness, (and) my transgression.
May the exalted one deliver, may the holy one love.
May the seven winds carry away my groaning. May
the worm lay it low, may the bird bear it upwards to
heaven. May a shoal of fish carry it away; may the
river bear it along. May the creeping thing of the field
come unto me; may the waters of the river as they flow
cleanse me. Enlighten me like a mask of gold. Food
and drink before thee perpetually may I get. Heap up
the worm, take away his life. The steps of thy altar,
thy many ones, may I ascend. With the worm make me
pass, and may I be kept with thee. Make me to be fed,
and may a favourable dream come. May the dream I
dream be favourable; may the dream I dream be
fulfilled. May the dream I dream turn to prosperity.
May Makhir, the god of dreams, settle upon my head.
Let me enter Beth-Saggil, the palace of the gods, the
temple of the lord. Give me unto Merodach, the
merciful, to prosperity, even unto prospering hands.

May thy entering (O Merodach) be exalted, may thy divinity be glorious ; may the men of thy city extol thy mighty deeds.'

Along with these prayers, the Assyrians possessed a collection of penitential psalms, which were composed at a very remote period in Southern Babylonia. The most perfect of those of which we have copies is the following :

My Lord is wroth in his heart: may he be appeased again.

May God be appeased again, for I knew not that I sinned.

May Istar, my mother, be appeased again, for I knew not that I sinned,

God knoweth that I knew not: may he be appeased.

Istar, my mother, knoweth that I knew not: may she be appeased.

May the heart of my God be appeased.

May God and Istar, my mother, be appeased.

May God cease from his anger.

May Istar, my mother, cease from her anger.

The transgression (I committed my God) knew.

[The next few lines are obliterated.]

The transgression (I committed, Istar, my mother, knew).

(My tears) I drink like the waters of the sea.

That which was forbidden by my God I ate without knowing.

That which was forbidden by Istar, my mother, I trampled on without knowing.

O my Lord, my transgression is great, many are my sins.

O my God, my transgression is great, many are my sins.

O Istar, my mother, my transgression is great, many are my sins.

O my God, who knowest that I knew not, my transgression is great, many are my sins.

O Istar, my mother, who knowest that I knew not, my transgression is great, many are my sins.

The transgression that I committed I knew not.

The sin that I sinned I knew not.

The forbidden thing did I eat.

The forbidden thing did I trample on.

My Lord, in the anger of his heart, has punished me.

God, in the strength of his heart, has taken me.

Istar, my mother, has seized upon me, and put me to grief.

God, who knoweth that I knew not, has afflicted me.

Istar, my mother, who knoweth that I knew not, has caused darkness.

I prayed, and none takes my hand. .

I wept, and none held my palm.

I cry aloud, but there is none that will hear me.

I am in darkness and hiding, I dare not look up.

To God I refer my distress, I utter my prayer.

The feet of Istar, my mother, I embrace.

To God, who knoweth that I knew not, my prayer I utter.

To Istar, my mother, who knoweth that I knew not, my prayer I address.

[The next four lines are destroyed.]

How long, O God (shall I suffer) ?

How long, O Istar, my mother (shall I be afflicted) ?

How long, O God, who knoweth that I knew not (shall I feel thy) strength ?

How long, O Istar, my mother, who knoweth that I knew
　　not, shall thy heart (be angry)?
Thou writest the number (?) of mankind, and none knoweth
　　it.
Thou callest man by his name, and what does he know?
Whether he shall be afflicted, or whether he shall be
　　prosperous, there is no man that knoweth.
O my God, thou givest not rest to thy servant.
In the waters of the raging flood take his hand.
The sin he has sinned turn into good.
Let the wind carry away the transgression I have committed.
Destroy my manifold wickednesses like a garment.
O my God, seven times seven are my transgressions, my
　　transgressions are (ever) before me.

A rubric is attached to this verse, stating that it is
to be repeated ten times, and at the end of the whole
psalm is the further rubric: 'For the tearful supplica-
tion of the heart let the glorious name of every god be
invoked sixty-five times, and then the heart shall have
peace.'

Reference is made in the psalm to the eating of forbidden foods, and we have other indications that certain
kinds of food, among which swine's flesh may be mentioned, were not allowed to be consumed. On particular
days also fasts were observed, and special days of fasting
and humiliation were prescribed in times of public
calamity. In the calendar of the Egibi banking firm,
the 2nd of Tammuz or June is entered as a day of
'weeping.' The institution of the Sabbath, moreover,

was known to the Babylonians and Assyrians, though
it was confounded with the feast of the new moon, since
it was kept, not every seven days, but on the seventh,
fourteenth, twenty-first, and twenty-eighth days of the
lunar month. On these days, we read in a sort of
Saints' calendar for the intercalary Elul : 'Flesh cooked
on the fire may not be eaten, the clothing of the body
may not be changed, white garments may not be put on,
a sacrifice may not be offered, the king may not ride in
his chariot, nor speak in public, the augur may not
mutter in a secret place, medicine of the body may not
be applied, nor may any curse be uttered.'   The very
name of Sabattu or Sabbath was employed by the
Assyrians, and is defined as 'a day of rest for the heart,'
while the Accadian equivalent is explained to mean 'a
day of completion of labour.'

So far as we are at present acquainted with the
peculiarities of the Assyro-Babylonian temple, it offers
many points of similarity to the temple of Solomon at
Jerusalem.   Thus there were an outer and an inner
court and a shrine, to which the priests alone had access.
In this was an altar approached by steps, as well as an
ark or coffer containing two inscribed tablets of stone,
such as were discovered by Mr. Rassam in the temple of
Balawât.   In the outer court was a large basin, filled
with water, and called 'a sea,' which was used for
ablutions and religious ceremonies.   At the entrance
stood colossal figures of winged bulls, termed 'cherubs,'
which were imagined to prevent the ingress of evil

spirits. Similar figures guarded the approach to the royal palace, and possibly to other houses as well. Some of them may now be seen in the British Museum. Within, the temples were filled with images of gods, great and small, which not only represented the deities whose names they bore, but were believed to confer of themselves a special sanctity on the place wherein they were placed. As among the Israelites, offerings were of two kinds, sacrifices and meal offerings. The sacrifice consisted of an animal, more usually a bullock, part of whose flesh was burnt upon the altar, while the rest was handed over to the priests or retained by the offerer. There is no trace of human sacrifices among the Assyrians, which is the more singular, since we learn that human sacrifice had been an Accadian institution. A passage in an old astrological work indicates that the victims were burnt to death, like the victims of Moloch ; and an early Accadian fragment expressly states that they were to be the children of those for whose sins they were offered to the gods. The fragment is as follows : 'The son who lifts his head among men, the son for his own life must the father) give; the head of the child for the head of the man must he give ; the neck of the child for the neck of the man must he give ; the breast of the child for the breast of the man must he give.' The idea of vicarious punishment is here clearly indicated.

The future life to which the Babylonian had looked forward was dreary enough. Hades, the land of the

dead, was beneath the earth, a place of darkness and
gloom, from which 'none might return,' where the spirits
of the dead flitted like bats, with dust alone for their
food.   Here the shadowy phantoms of the heroes of old
time sat crowned, each upon his throne, a belief to which
allusion is made by the Hebrew prophet in his prophecy of the coming overthrow of Babylon (Is. xiv. 9).
In the midst stood the palace of Allat, the queen of the
underworld, where the waters of life bubbled forth
beside the golden throne of the spirits of earth, restoring
those who might drink of them to life and the upper air.
The entrance to this dreary abode of the departed lay
beyond Datilla, the river of death, at the mouth of the
Euphrates, and it was here that the hero Gisdhubar
saw Xisuthros, the Chaldean Noah, after his translation
to the fields of the blessed.   In later times, when the
horizon of geographical knowledge was widened, the
entrance to the gloomy world of Hades, and the earthly
paradise that was above it, were alike removed to other
and more unknown regions.   The conception of the
after-life, moreover, was made brighter, at all events, for
the favoured few.   An Assyrian court poet prays thus
on behalf of his king: 'The land of the silver sky, oil
unceasing, the benefits of blessedness may he obtain
among the feasts of the gods. and a happy cycle among
their light, even life everlasting, and bliss; such is my
prayer to the gods who dwell in the land of Assur.'
Even at a far earlier time we find the great Chaldean epic
of Gisdhubar concluding with a description of the bliss-

ful lot of the spirit of Ea-bani : 'On a couch he reclines and pure water he drinks. Him who is slain in battle thou seest and I see. His father and his mother support) his head, his wife addresses the corpse. His friends in the fields are standing ; thou seest them) and I see. His spoil on the ground is uncovered ; of his spoil he hath no oversight, (as) thou seest and I see. His tender orphans beg for bread ; the food that was stored in (his) tent is eaten.' Here the spirit of Ea-bani is supposed to behold from his couch in heaven the deeds that take place on the earth below.

Heaven itself had not always been 'the land of the silver sky' of later Assyrian belief. The Babylonians once believed that the gods inhabited the snow-clad peak of Rowandiz, 'the mountain of the world' and 'the mountain of the East,' as it was also termed, which supported the starry vault of heaven. It is to this old Babylonian belief that allusion is made in Isaiah xiv. 13, 14, where the Babylonian monarch is represented as saying in his heart : 'I will ascend into heaven, I will exalt my throne above the stars of God : I will sit also on the mount of the assembly (of the gods)[1] in the extremities[2] of the north : I will ascend above the heights of the clouds.'

As in all old forms of heathen faith, religion and mythology were inextricably mixed together. Myths were told of most of the gods. Reference has already been made to the myth of Istar and Tammuz, the pro-

---

[1] A. V 'congregation.'　　　　　　　　[2] A V. 'sides.'

totype of the Greek legend of Aphroditê and Adonis.
So, too, the Greek story of the theft of fire by Prometheus has its parallel in the Babylonian story of the god
Zu, 'the divine storm-bird,' who stole the lightning of
Bel, the tablet whereon the knowledge of futurity is
written, and who was punished for his crime by the father
of the gods. In reading the legend of the plague-demon
Lubara, whom Anu sends to smite the evildoers in
Babylon, Erech, and other places, we are reminded of
the avenging angel of God whom David saw standing
with a drawn sword over Jerusalem.

One of the most curious of the Babylonian myths was
that which told how the seven evil-spirits or storm-
demons had once warred against the moon and threat
ened to devour it. Samas and Istar fled from the lower
sky, and the Moon-god would have been blotted out
from heaven had not Bel and Ea sent Merodach in his
'glistening armour' to rescue him. The myth is really
a primitive attempt to explain a lunar eclipse, and finds
its illustration in the dragon of the Chinese, who is still
popularly believed by them to devour the sun or moon
when an eclipse takes place.

The primæval victory of light and order over darkness and chaos, which seems to be repeated whenever
the sun bursts through a storm-cloud, was similarly
expressed in a mythical form. It was the victory of
Merodach over Tiamat, 'the deep,' the personification of
chaos and elemental anarchy. The myth was embodied
in a poem, the greater part of which has been preserved

to us. We are told how Merodach was armed by the
gods with bow and scimetar, how alone he faced and
fought the dragon Tiamat, driving the winds into her
throat when she opened her mouth to swallow him, and
how, finally, he cut open her body, scattering in flight
'the rebellious deities' who had stood at her side.
Tiamat, or the watery chaos, is usually represented with
wings, claws, tail, and horns, but she is also identified
with 'the wicked serpent' of 'night and darkness,' 'the
monstrous serpent of seven heads,' 'which beats the sea.'

The most interesting of the old myths and traditions
of Babylonia are those in which we can trace, more or
less clearly, the lineaments of the accounts of the
creation of the world and the early history of man,
given us in the early chapters of Genesis. There was
more than one legend of the creation. In a text which
came from the library of Cuthah, it was described as
taking place on evolutionary principles, the first created
beings being the brood of chaos, men with 'the bodies
of birds' and 'the faces of ravens,' who were succeeded
by the more perfect forms of the existing world. But
the library of Assur-bani-pal also contained an account
of the creation, which bears a remarkable resemblance
to that in the first chapter of Genesis. Unfortunately,
however, it seems to have been of Assyrian and not
Babylonian origin, and, therefore, not to have been of
early date. In this account the creation appears to be
described as having been accomplished in six days. It
begins in these words :

' At that time the heavens above named not a name,
nor did the earth below record one ; yea, the ocean was
their first creator, the flood of the deep  Tiamat) was
she who bore them all.   Their waters were embosomed
in one place, and the clouds (?) were not collected, the
plant was still ungrown.   At that time the gods had not
issued forth, any one of them ; by no name were they
recorded, no destiny (had they fixed).   Then the (great)
gods were made ; Lakhmu and Lakhamu issued forth
the first.   They grew up.   .   .   .   Next were made the
host of heaven and earth.   The time was long, (and
then) the gods Anu, (Bel, and Ea were born of) the host
of heaven and earth.'   The rest of the account is lost,
and it is not until we come to the fifth tablet of the
series, which describes the appointment of the heavenly
bodies, that the narrative is again preserved.   Here we
are told that the creator, who seems to have been Ea,
' made the stations of the great gods, even the stars,
fixing the places of the principal stars like   .   .   .   .
He ordered the year, setting over it the decans ; yea, he
established three stars for each of the twelve months.'
It will be remembered that, according to Genesis, the
appointment of the heavenly bodies to guide and govern
the seasons was the work of the fourth day, and since
the work is described in the fifth tablet or book of the
Assyrian account, while the first tablet describes the
condition of the universe before the creation was begun,
it becomes probable that the Assyrians also knew that
the work was performed on the fourth day.   The next

tablet states that 'at that time the gods in their assembly created (the living creatures). They made the mighty (animals). They caused the living beings to come forth, the cattle of the field, the beast of the field, and the creeping thing.' Unfortunately the rest of the narrative is in too mutilated a condition for a translation to be possible, and the part which describes the creation of man has not yet been recovered among the ruins of the library of Nineveh.

The Chaldean account of the Deluge was discovered by Mr. George Smith, and its close resemblance to the account in Genesis is well known. Those who wish to see a translation of it, according to the latest researches, will find one in the pages of 'Fresh Light from the Ancient Monuments.' The account was introduced as an episode into the eleventh book of the great Babylonian epic of Gisdhubar, and appears to be the amalgamation of two older poems on the subject. The story of the Deluge, in fact, was a favourite theme among the Babylonians, and we have fragments of at least two other versions of it, neither of which, however, agree so remarkably with the Biblical narrative as does the version discovered by Mr. Smith. Apart from the profound difference caused by the polytheistic character of the Chaldean account, and the monotheism of the Scriptural narrative, it is only in details that the two accounts vary from one another. Thus, the vessel in which Xisuthros, the Chaldean Noah, sails, is a ship, guided by a steersman, and not an ark, and others

F

besides his own family are described as being admitted
into it. So, too, the period of time during which the
flood was at its height is said to have been seven days
only, while, beside the raven and the dove, Xisuthros is
stated to have sent out a third bird, the swallow, in
order to determine how far the waters had subsided.
The Chaldean ark rested, moreover, on Rowandiz, the
highest of the mountains of Eastern Kurdistan, and
the peak whereon Accadian mythology imagined the
heavens to be supported, and not on the northern or
Armenian continuation of the range. Babylonian tradition, too, had fused into one Noah and Enoch, Xisuthros
being represented as translated to the land of immor-
tality immediately after his descent from the ark and
his sacrifice to the gods. It is noticeable that the
Chaldean account agrees with that of the Bible in one
remarkable respect, in which it differs from almost all
the other traditions of the Deluge found throughout the
world. This is in its ascribing the cause of the Deluge
to the wickedness of mankind. It was sent as a punishment for sin.

As might have been expected, the Babylonians and
Assyrians knew of the building of the Tower of Babel,
and the dispersion of mankind. Men had 'turned
against the father of all the gods,' under a leader the
thoughts of whose heart 'were evil.' At Babylon they
began to erect ' a mound,' or hill-like tower, but the
winds destroyed it in the night, and Anu 'confounded
great and small on the mound,' as well as their 'speech,'

and ' made strange their counsel.' All this was supposed
to have taken place at the time of the autumnal equinox,
and it is possible that the name of the rebel leader,
which is lost, was Etána. At all events the demi-god
Etána played a conspicuous part in the early historical
mythology of Babylonia, like two other famous divine
kings, Ner and Dun, and a fragment describes him as
having built a city of brick. However this may be,
Etána is the Babylonian Titan of Greek writers, who,
with Prometheus and Ogygos, made war against the
gods.

If we sum up the character of Assyrian religion, we
shall find it characterised by curious contrasts. On the
one hand we shall find it grossly polytheistic, believing
in 'lords many and gods many,' and admitting not only
gods and demi-gods, and even deified men, but the
multitudinous spirits, 'the host of heaven and earth,'
who were classed together as the ' 300 spirits of heaven
and the 600 spirits of earth.' Some of these were
beneficent, others hostile, to man. In addition to this
vast army of divine powers, the Assyrian offered worship
also to the heavenly bodies, and to the spirits of rivers
and mountains. He even set up stones or ' Beth-els,' so
called because they were imagined to be veritable
'houses of god,' wherein the godhead dwelt, and over
these he poured out libations of oil and wine. Yet, on
the other hand, with all this gross polytheism, there was
a strong tendency to monotheism. The supreme god,
Assur, is often spoken of in language which at first sight

seems monotheistic: to him the Assyrian monarchs
ascribe their victories, and in his name they make war
against the unbeliever. A similar inconsistency prevailed
in the character of Assyrian worship itself. There was
much in it which commands our admiration: the
Assyrian confessed his sins to his gods, he begged
for their pardon and help, he allowed nothing to
interfere with what he conceived to be his religious
duties. With all this, his worship of Istar was stained
with the foulest excesses  excesses, too, indulged in,
like those of the Phœnicians, in the name and for the
sake of religion.

Much of this inconsistency may be explained by the
history of his religious ideas. As we have seen, a large
part of them was derived from a non-Semitic population,
the primitive inhabitants of Babylonia, under whose
influence the Semitic Babylonians had come at a time
when they still lacked nearly all the elements of culture.
The result was a form of creed in which the old
Accadian faith was bodily taken over by an alien race,
but at the same time profoundly modified. It was
Accadian religion interpreted by the Semitic mind and
belief. Baal worship, which saw the Sun-god everywhere
under an infinite variety of manifestations, waged a
constant struggle with the conceptions of the borrowed
creed, but never overcame them altogether. The gods
and spirits of the Accadians remained to the last, although
permeated and overlaid with the worship of the Semitic
Sun-god. As time went on, new religious elements were

introduced, and Assyro-Babylonian religion underwent new phases, while in Assyria itself the deified state in the person of the god Assur tended to absorb the religious cult and aspirations of the people. The higher minds of the nation struggled now and again towards the conception of one supreme God and of a purer form of faith, but the dead weight of polytheistic beliefs and practices prevented them from ever really reaching it. In the best examples of their religious literature we constantly fall across expressions and ideas which show how wide was the gulf that separated them from that kindred people of Israel to whom the oracles of God were revealed.

# CHAPTER IV.

## ART, LITERATURE, AND SCIENCE.

ASSYRIAN art was, speaking generally, imported from Babylonia. Even the palace of the king was built of bricks, and raised upon a mound like the palaces and temples of Babylonia, although stone was plentiful in Assyria, and there was no marshy plain where inundations might be feared. It was only the walls that were lined with sculptured slabs of alabaster, the sculptures taking the place of the paintings in vermilion, which adorned the houses of Babylonia (Ezek. xxiii. 14).

It is at Khorsabad, or Dur-Sargon, the city built by Sargon, to the north of Nineveh, that we can best study the architectural genius of Assyria. The city was laid out in the form of a square, and surrounded by walls forty-six feet thick and over a mile in length each way, the angles of which faced the four cardinal points. The outer wall was flanked with eight tall towers, and was erected on a mound of rubble.

On the north-west side stood the royal palace, defended also by a wall of its own, and built on a T-shaped platform. It was approached through an outer court, the gates of which were hung under arches of enamelled brick, and guarded by colossal figures in stone. From the court an inclined plane led to the first terrace, occupied by a number of small rooms, in which the French excavators saw the barracks of the palace-guard. Above this terrace rose a second, at a height of about ten feet, upon which was built the royal palace itself. This was entered through a gateway, on either side of which stood the stone figure of a 'cherub,' while within it was a court 350 feet long and 170 feet wide. Beyond this court was an inner one, which formed a square of 150 feet. On its left were the royal chambers, consisting of a suite of ten rooms, and beyond them again the private chapel of the monarch, leading to the apartments in which he commonly lived. On the west side of the palace rose a tower, built in stages, on the summit of which was the royal observatory.

It is a question whether the Assyrian palace possessed any upper stories. On the whole, probability speaks against it. Columns, however, were used plentifully. The column, in fact, had been a Babylonian invention, and originated in the necessity of supporting buildings on wooden pillars in a country where there was no stone. From Babylonia columnar architecture passed into Assyria, where it assumed exaggerated forms, the column being sometimes made to rest on the backs of lions, dogs, and winged bulls.

The apertures which served as windows were protected by heavy folds of tapestry, that kept out the heats of summer and the cold winds of winter. In warm weather, however, the inmates of the house preferred to sic in the open air, either in the airy courts upon which its chambers opened, or under the shady trees of the *paradeisos* or park attached to the dwellings of the rich. The leases of houses let or sold in Nineveh in the time of the Second Assyrian Empire generally make mention of the 'shrubbery,' which formed part of the property.

Assyrian sculpture was for the most part in relief. The Assyrians carved badly in the round, unlike the Babylonians, some of whose sitting statues are not wanting in an air of dignity and repose. But they excelled in that kind of shallow relief of which so many examples have been brought to the British Museum. We can trace three distinct periods in the history of this form of art. The first period is that which begins, so far as we know at present, with the age of Assur-natsir-pal. It is characterised by boldness and vigour, by an absence of background or landscape, and by an almost total want of perspective. With very few exceptions, faces and figures are drawn in profile. But with all this want of skill, the work is often striking from the spirit with which it is executed, and the naturalness with which animals, more especially, are depicted. A bas-relief representing a lion-hunt of Assur-natsir-pal has been often selected as a typical, though favourable, illustration of the art of this age.

The second period extends from the foundation of the Second Assyrian Empire to the reign of Esar-haddon. The artist has lost in vigour, but has compensated for it by care and accuracy. The foreground is now filled in with vegetable and other forms, all drawn with a pre-Raffaellite exactitude. The relief consequently becomes exceedingly rich, and produces the effect of embroidery in stone. It is probable that the delicate minuteness of this period of art was in great measure due to the work in ivory that had now become fashionable at Nineveh.

The third, and best period, is that of the reign of Assur bani-pal. There is a return to the freedom of the first period, but without its accompanying rudeness and want of skill. The landscape is either left bare, or indicated in outline only, the attention of the spectator being thus directed to the principal sculpture itself. The delineation of the human figure has much improved ; vegetable forms have lost much of their stiffness, and we meet with several examples of successful foreshortening. Up to the last, however, the Assyrian artist succeeded but badly in human portraiture. Nothing can surpass some of his pictures of animals ; when he came to deal with the human figure he expended his strength on embroidered robes and the muscles of the legs and arms. The reason of this is not difficult to discover. Unlike the Egyptian, who excelled in the delineation of the human form, he did not draw from nude models. The details of the drapery were with him of more importance than the features of the face or the posture of the limbs. We cannot expect to find portraits in the sculptures of Assyria. Little, if any, attempt is made even to distinguish the natives of different foreign countries from one another, except in

the way of dress.    All alike have the same features as
the Assyrians themselves.

The effect of the bas-reliefs was enhanced by the
red, black, blue, and white colours with which they were
picked out.  The practice had come from Babylonia,
but whereas the Babylonians delighted in brilliant
colouring, their northern neighbours contented themselves with much more sober hues.  It was no doubt
from the populations of Mesopotamia that the Greeks
first learnt to paint and tint their sculptured stone.
Unfortunately it is difficult, if not impossible, to find
any trace of colouring remaining in the Assyrian bas-
reliefs now in Europe.  When first disinterred, however,
the colours were still bright in many cases, although
exposure to the air soon caused them to fade and
perish.

The bas-reliefs and colossi were moved from the
quarries out of which they had been dug, or the workshops
in which they had been carved, by the help of sledges
and rollers.  Hundreds of captives were employed to
drag the huge mass along; sometimes it was transported by water, the boat on which it lay being pulled
by men on shore; sometimes it was drawn over the
land by gangs of slaves, urged to their work by the rod
and sword of their task-masters.  On the colossus itself
stood an overseer holding to his mouth what looks on
the monument like a modern speaking-trumpet.  Over
a sculpture representing the transport of one of these
colossi Sennacherib has engraved the words: 'Senna-

Fragment now in the British Museum showing primitive Hieroglyphics and Cuneiform Characters side by side.

cherib, king of legions, king of Assyria, has caused the
winged bull and the colossi, the divinities which were
made in the land of the city of the Baladians, to be
brought with joy to the palace of his lordship, which is
within Nineveh.' We may infer from this epigraph that
the images themselves were believed to be in some way
the abode of divinity, like the Beth-els or sacred stones
to which reference has been made in the last chapter

Like Assyrian art, Assyrian literature was for the
most part derived from Babylonia. A large portion of
it was translated from Accadian originals. Sometimes
the original was lost or forgotten ; more frequently it
was re-edited from time to time with interlinear or
parallel translations in Assyro-Babylonian. This was
more especially the case with the sacred texts, in which
the old language of Accad was itself accounted sacred,
like Latin in the services of the Roman Catholic Church,
or Coptic in those of the modern Egyptian Church.

The Accadians had been the inventors of the hieroglyphics or pictorial characters out of which the
cuneiform characters had afterwards grown. Writing
begins with pictures, and the writing of the Babylonians
formed no exception to the rule. The pictures were at
first painted on the papyrus leaves which grew in the
marshes of the Euphrates, but as time went on a new and
more plentiful writing material came to be employed in
the shape of clay. Clay was literally to be found under
the feet of every one. All that was needed was to
impress it, while still wet, with the hieroglyphic pictures,

and then dry it in the sun. It is probable that the bricks used in the construction of the great buildings of Chaldea were first treated in this way. At all events we find that up to the last, the Babylonian kings stamped their names and titles in the middle of such bricks, and hundreds of them may be met with in the museums of Europe bearing the name of Nebuchadnezzar. When once the discovery was made that clay could be employed as a writing material, it was quickly turned to good account. All Babylonia began to write on tablets of clay, and though papyrus continued to be used, it was reserved for what we should now term 'éditions de luxe.' The writing instrument had originally been the edge of a stone or a piece of stick, but these were soon superseded by a metal stylus with a square head. Under the combined influence of the clay tablet and the metal stylus, the old picture-writing began to degenerate into the cuneiform or 'wedge-shaped' characters with which the monuments of Assyria have made us familiar. It was difficult, if not impossible, any longer to draw circles and curves, and accordingly angles took the place of circles, and straight lines the place of curves. Continuous lines were equally difficult to form; it was easier to represent them by a series of indentations, each of which took a wedge-like appearance from the square head of the stylus. As soon as the exact forms of the old pictures began to be obliterated, other alterations became inevitable. The forms began to be simplified by the omission of lines or wedges which were no longer necessary, now that the character had become a mere symbol instead of a picture; and this process of simplification went on from one century to another, until in many instances the later form of a character is hardly more than a shadow of what it originally was. Education was widely spread in Babylonia; in spite of the cumbrousness and intricacy of the system of writing there were few, it would appear, who could not read and write and hence, as was natural, all kinds of handwritings were prevalent, some good and some bad. Among these various cursive or running hands were some which were selected for public documents; but as the hands varied, not only among individuals, but also from age to age, the official script never became fixed and permanent, but changed constantly, each change, however, bringing with it increased simplicity in the shapes of the characters, and a greater departure from the primitive hieroglyphic form. The earliest contemporaneous monuments with which we are at present acquainted, are those recently excavated by the French Consul M. de Sarzec at a place called Tel Loh; on these we see the early pictures in the very act of passing into cuneiform characters, the pictures being sometimes preserved and sometimes already lost. A comparison of the forms found at Tel-Loh with those usually employed in the time of Nebuchadnezzar, will show at a glance what profound modifications were undergone by the cuneiform syllabary in the course of its transmission from generation to generation.

In contrast to the Babylonians, the Assyrians were a nation of warriors and huntsmen, not of students, and with them, therefore, a knowledge of writing was confined to a particular class, that of the scribes. At an early period, accordingly, in the history of the kingdom, a special form of script was adopted not only in official documents, but in private documents as well, and this script remained practically unchanged down to the fall of Nineveh. This form of script was one of the many simplified forms of handwriting that were used in Babylonia, and it was fortunately a very clear and well-defined one. Now and then, it is true, contact with Babylonia made an Assyrian king desirous of imitating the archaic writing of Babylonia, and inscriptions were consequently engraved in florid characters, abounding in a multiplicity of needless wedges, and reminding us of our modern black-letter. Such ornamental inscriptions are not numerous, and were carved only on stone. The clay literature was all written in the ordinary Assyrian characters, except when the scribe was unable to recognise a character in a Babylonian text he was copying, and so reproduced it exactly in his copy.

The clay tablets used by the Assyrians were an improvement on those of Babylonia. Instead of being merely dried in the sun, they were thoroughly baked in a kiln, holes being drilled through them here and there to allow the steam to escape. As a rule, therefore, the tablets of Assyria are smaller than those of Babylonia, since there was always a danger of a large tablet being

AN ASSYRIAN BOOK.
(*From the original in the British Museum.*)

broken in the fire. In consequence of the small size of the tablets, and the amount of text with which it was often necessary to cover them, the characters impressed upon them are frequently minute, so minute, indeed, as to suggest that they must have been written with the help of a magnifying glass. This supposition is confirmed by the existence of a magnifying lens of crystal discovered by Sir A. H. Layard on the site of the library of Nineveh, and now in the British Museum.

A literary people like the Babylonians needed libraries, and libraries were accordingly established at a very early period in all the great cities of the country, and plentifully stocked with books in papyrus and clay. In imitation of these Babylonian libraries, libraries were also founded in Assyria by the Assyrian kings. There was a library at Assur, and another at Calah which seems to have been as old as the city itself. But the chief library of Assyria that, in fact, from which most of the Assyrian literature we possess has come, was the great library of Nineveh (Kouyunjik). This owed its magnitude and reputation to Assur-bani-pal, who filled it with copies of the plundered books of Babylonia. A whole army of scribes was employed in it, busily engaged in writing and editing old texts. Assur-bani-pal is never weary of telling us, in the colophon at the end of the last tablet of a series which made up a single work, that 'Nebo and Tasmit had given him broad ears and enlightened his eyes so as to see the engraved characters of the written tablets, whereof none of the kings that had gone before had seen this text, the wisdom of Nebo, all the literature of the library that exists,' so that he had 'written, engraved, and explained it on tablets, and placed it within his palace for the inspection of readers.'

A good deal of the literature was of a lexical and grammatical kind, and was intended to assist the Semitic student in interpreting the old Accadian texts. Lists of characters were drawn up with their pronunciation in Accadian and the translation into Assyrian of the words represented by them. Since the Accadian pronunciation of a character was frequently the phonetic value attached to it by the Assyrians, these syllabaries, as they have been termed in consequence of the fact that the cuneiform characters denoted syllables and not letters—have been of the greatest possible assistance in the decipherment of the inscriptions. Besides the syllabaries, the Semitic scribes compiled tables of Accadian words and grammatical forms with their Assyro-Babylonian equivalents, as well as lists of the names of animals, birds, reptiles, fish, stones, vegetables, medicines, and the like in the two languages. There are even geographical and astronomical lists, besides long lists of Assyrian synonyms and the titles of military and civil officers.

Other tablets contain phrases and sentences extracted from some particular Accadian work and explained in Assyrian, while others again are exercises or reading-books intended for boys at school, who were learning

the old dead language of Chaldea. In addition to
these helps whole texts were provided with Assyrian
translations, sometimes interlinear, sometimes placed in
a parallel column on the right-hand side ; so that it
is not wonderful that the Assyrians now and then
attempted to write in the extinct Accadian, just as we
write nowadays in Latin, though in both cases, it must
be confessed, not always with success.

Accadian, however, was not the only language besides
his own that the Semitic Babylonian or Assyrian was
required to know. Aramaic had become the common
language of trade and diplomacy, so that not only was
it assumed by the ministers of Hezekiah that an official
like the Rab-shakeh or Vizier of Sennacherib could
speak it as a matter of course (2 Kings xviii. 26),
but even in trading documents we find the Aramaic
language and alphabet used side by side with the
Assyrian cuneiform. This common use of Aramaic
explains how it was that the Jews after the Babylonish
captivity gave up their own language in favour not of
the Assyro-Babylonian, but of the Aramaic of Northern
Syria and Arabia. An educated Assyrian was thus
expected to be able to read and write a dead language,
Accadian, and to read, write, and speak a foreign living
language, Aramaic. In addition to these languages,
moreover, he took an interest in others which were
spoken by his neighbours around him. The Rab-
shakeh of Sennacherib was able to speak Hebrew, and
tablets have been discovered giving the Assyrian

renderings of lists of words from the barbarous dialects
of the Kossæans in the mountains of Elam and of the
Semitic nomads on the western side of the Euphrates.

All the branches of knowledge known at the time
were treated of in Assyrian literature, though naturally
history, legend, and poetry occupied a prominent place
in it. But even such subjects as the despatches of
generals in the field, or the copies of royal corre-
spondence found a place in the public library. The
chronology of Assyria, and therewith of the Old
Testament also, has been restored by means of the lists
of successive 'eponyms' or officers after whom the
years were named, while a recent discovery has brought
to light a table of Semitic Babylonian kings, arranged
in dynasties, which traces them back to B.C. 2330.

A flood of light has been poured on Chaldean
astronomy and astrology, by the fragments of the
original work called 'The Observations of Bel' which was
translated into Greek by the Babylonian priest Bêrôssos.
It consisted of seventy-two books, and was compiled
for king Sargon of Accad, whose date is assigned by
Nabonidos to B.C. 3800. Another work on omens, in
137 books, had been compiled for the same king, and
both remained to the last days of the Assyrian Empire
the standard treatises on the subjects with which they
dealt. To the same period we should probably refer a
treatise on agriculture, extracts from which have been
preserved in a reading-book in Accadian and Assyrian.
Here the songs are quoted with which the Accadian

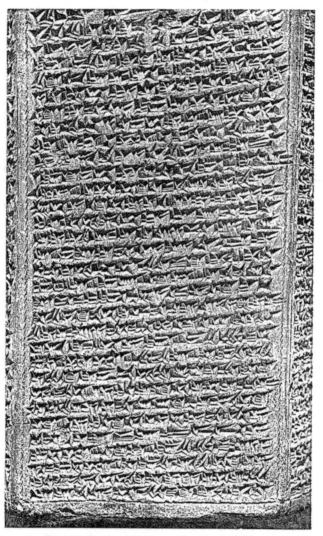

Part of an Assyrian Cylinder containing Hezekiah's Name.

*(From the original in the British Museum.)*

The following is the transcription into the ordinary Assyrian Characters of the last thirteen lines of the photograph on page 104.

29.
30.
31.
32.
33.
34.
35.
36.
37.
38.
39.
40.
41.

W.A.I., I, 39, Col. III, 29 41.

By way of comparison, a specimen of Babylonian writing is also given here.

SPECIMEN OF BABYLONIAN WRITING FROM AN INSCRIPTION OF
NEBUCHADNEZZAR.

The following is the transliteration and translation of the transcription on page 105.

29.    a-na   D P.*   Kha-za-ki-ya-hu
       *to*            *Hezekiah.*

30.  D.P.    Ya-hu-da-â    id-di-nu-su    nak-ris    a-na    zil-li    e-sir-su
     *of the Jews they gave him as an enemy    In a dungeon he shut him up.*

31.  ip-lukh    lab-ba-su-un    sarrani    mat    Mu-tsu-ri
     *Their heart feared.    The kings of the country of Egypt,*

32.  D.P. tsabi  D.P. miti ani  D.P. narkabaté  D.P. sisê  sa  sar  D.P. Me-lukh-khi
     *the men of    bows and    chariots,    the horses of the king of    Meluhh,*

33.  e-mu-ki    la    ni-bi    ik-te-ru-nim-ma    il-li-ku
     *a force without number    they brought together and they marched to*

---

* D.P. stands for 'Determinative Prefix.' There are thirty determinatives in Assyrian.
The D.P. ⟶, the sign meaning 'heaven,' or anything in heaven, is put before the name of a god.
The D.P. ⟨, the sign meaning 'country,' is put before the name of a country.
The D.P. ⟨, the sign meaning 'city,' is put before the name of a city, and so on

34. ri-tsu-uś-śu-un.    i-na    ta-mir-ti    D.P. Al-ta-ḳu-u    it-ti-su-un
their aid.    In the sight of the city    Altaku    with them

35. el-la-mu-u-a    ši-id-ru    rit-ku-nu    u-sa-a' lu
before me the order of battle they had placed, they appealed to

36. D.P. kakk-su-un    i-na    tukulti    D.P. Assur    beli-ya
their weapons.    By the support of Assur    my lord

37. am-da-khi-its-ma    as-ta kan    hapikta-su-un
I fought and I accomplished their overthrow;

38. D.P. beli-narkabate    u    abli    sarrani    D.P. Mu-tsu-ra-â
the charioteers and the sons of the kings of the Egyptians

39. a-di    D.P. beli-narkabate    sa    sar    D.P. Me-lukh khi    bal-ḏu-śu-un
together with the charioteers of the king of    Meluḫḫi    alive

40. i-na    ḳabal    tam-kha-ri    ik-su da    ḳata    D.P. Al-ta-ḳu-u
in the midst of battle my two hands captured.    The city Altaku

41. D.P. Ta-am-na-a    al-me    aks-ud    as-lu-la    sal la-šun
and the city Tâmnâ    I besieged I captured I carried away their spoil.

ox-drivers beguiled their labours in the field : 'An heifer am I : to the cow thou art yoked : the plough's handle is strong : lift it up lift it up ;' or again : 'The knees are marching, the feet are not resting ; with no wealth of thy own grain thou begettest for me.' Some of the most curious specimens of this department of literature are the fables, riddles, and proverbs, which embody the homely wisdom of the unofficial classes.

Here, for instance, is a riddle propounded to Nergal and the other gods by 'the wise man,' such as Orientals still delight in :

'What is (found) in the house ; what is (concealed) in the secret place ; what is (fixed) in the foundation of the house ; what exists on the floor of the house ; what is (perceived) in the lower part (of the house) ; what goes down by the sides of the house ; what in the ditch of the house (makes) broad furrows ; what roars like a bull ; what brays like an ass ; what flutters like a sail ; what bleats like a sheep ; what barks like a dog ; what growls like a bear ; what enters into a man ; what enters into a woman ?' The answer is, of course, the air or wind.

Among the most treasured portions of the library of Nineveh was the poetical literature, comprising epics, hymns to the gods, psalms and songs. Fifteen of these songs, we are told, were arranged on the eastern and northern sides of the building, 'on the western side being nine songs to Assur, Bel the voice of the firmament, the Southern Sun,' and another god. The mention of songs to Assur shows that there were some

which were of Assyrian origin.   The epics, however, all
came from Babylonia, and were partly translations from
Accadian, partly independent compositions of Semitic
Babylonian poets.   The names of the reputed authors
of many of them have come down to us.   Thus the
great epic of Gisdhubar was ascribed to Sin liki-unnini;
the legend of Etana to Nis-Sin; the fable of the fox to
Ru-Merodach the son of Nitakh-Dununa.

The epic of Gisdhubar, as has already been stated,
contained the account of the Deluge, introduced as an
episode into the eleventh book.   It consisted in all of
twelve books, and was arranged upon an astronomical
principle, the subject-matter of each of the books being
made to correspond with one of the signs of Zodiac.
Thus the fifth book records the death of a monstrous
lion at the hands of Gisdhubar, answering to the
Zodiacal Leo; in the sixth book the hero is vainly
wooed by Istar, the Virgo of the Zodiacal signs; and
just as Aquarius is in the eleventh Zodiacal sign, so the
history of the Deluge is embodied in the eleventh book.
There was a special reason, however, for this arrange-
ment; Gisdhubar himself was a solar hero.   He seems
originally to have been the fire-stick of the primitive
Accadians, and then the god or spirit of the fire it
produced, eventually in the Semitic period passing first
into a form of the Sun-god, and then into a solar hero.
His twelve labours or adventures answer to the twelve
months of the year through which the sun moves, like
the twelve labours of the Greek Hêraklês.   The latter,

indeed, were simply the twelve labours of Gisdhubar transported to the west. The Greeks received many myths and mythological conceptions from the Phœnicians, along with their early culture, and these myths had themselves been brought by the Phœnicians from their original home in Chaldea. It has long been recognised that Hêraklês was the borrowed Phœnician Sun-god; we now know that his primitive prototype had been adopted by the Phœnicians from the Accadians of Babylonia  It is not strange, therefore, that just as in the Greek myth of Aphrodîtê and Adônis we find the outlines of the old Chaldean story of Istar and Tammuz, so in the legends of Hêraklês we find an echo of the legends of Gisdhubar. The lion destroyed by Gisdhubar is the lion of Nemea; the winged bull made by Anu to avenge the slight offered to Istar is the winged bull of Krete; the tyrant Khumbaba, slain by Gisdhubar in 'the land of pine-trees, the seat of the gods, the sanctuary of the spirits' is the tyrant Geryôn; the gems borne by the trees of the forest beyond 'the gateway of the sun' are the apples of the Hesperides; and the deadly sickness of Gisdhubar himself is but the fever sent by the poisoned tunic of Nessos through the veins of the Greek hero. It is curious thus to trace to their first source the myths which have made so deep an impress on classical art and literature. The indebtedness of European culture to the valley of the Euphrates is becoming more and more apparent every year.

It is impossible to determine the age of the great

Chaldean epic, but it must have been composed subsequently to the period when, through the precession of the equinoxes, Aries came to be the first sign of the Zodiac instead of Taurus, that is to say, about B.C. 2500. On the other hand, it is difficult to make it later than B.C. 2000, while the whole character and texture of the poem shows that it has been put together from older lays, which have been united into a single whole. The poem deservedly continued to be a favourite among the Babylonians and Assyrians, and more than one edition of it was made for the library of Assur bani-pal. A translation of all the portions of it that have been discovered will be found in George Smith's 'Chaldean Account of Genesis.'

It is difficult for the English reader to appreciate justly the real character of many of these old poems. The tablets on which they are inscribed were broken in pieces when Nineveh was destroyed, and the roof of the library fell in upon them. A text, therefore, has generally to be pieced together from a number of fragments, leaving gaps and lacunæ which mar the pleasure of reading it. Then, again, the translator frequently comes across a word or phrase which is new to him, and which he is consequently obliged to leave untranslated or to render purely conjecturally. At times there is a lacuna in the original text itself. When the Assyrian scribe was unable to read the tablet he was copying, either because the characters had been effaced by time or because their Babylonian forms were unknown to him,

he wrote the word *khibi,* 'it is wanting,' and left a blank
in his text    It is not wonderful, therefore, that what is
really a fine piece of literature reads tamely and poorly
in its English dress, more especially when we remember
that the decipherer is compelled to translate literally,
and cannot have recourse to those idiomatic paraphrases
which are permissible when we are dealing with known
languages

But it must be confessed that many of the best compositions of Babylonia are spoilt for us by the references
to a puerile superstition, and the ever-present dread of
witchcraft and magic which they contain.  A good
example of this curious mixture of exalted thought and
debasing superstition is the following hymn to the Sun-
god :—

'O Sun-god, king of heaven and earth, director of things above
        and below,
    O Sun god, thou that clothest the dead with life, delivered by
        thy hands,
    judge unbribed, director of mankind,
    supreme in mercy for him that is in trouble,
    bidding the child and offspring come forth, light of the world,
    creator of all thy land, the Sun god art thou !
    O Sun god, when the bewitchment for many days
    is bound behind me and there is no deliverer,
    the expulsion of the curse and return of health are brought
        about (by thee).
    Among mankind, the flock of the god Ner, whatever be their
        names, he selects me :

                                          **H**

after trouble he fills me with rest,

and day and night I stand undarkened.

In the anguish of my heart and the sickness of my body there
is . . .

O father supreme, I am debased and walk to and fro.

In misery and affliction I held myself (?).

My littleness (?) I know not, the sin I have committed I knew
not.

I am small and he is great :

The walls of my god may I pass.

O bird stand still and hear the hound !

O Sun-god stand still and hear me !

The name of the evil bewitchment that has been brought
about overpower,

whether the bewitchment of my father, or the bewitchment of
my begetter,

or the bewitchment of the seven branches of the house of my
father,

or the bewitchment of my family and my slaves,

or the bewitchment of my free-born women and concubines,

or the bewitchment of the dead and the living, or the bewitchment of the adult and the suckling (?),

or the bewitchment of my father and of him who is not my
father.

To father and mother be thou a father, and to brother and
child be thou a father.

To friend and neighbour be thou a father, and to handmaid
and man be thou a father.

To the field thou hast made and thy . . . be thou a
father.

May the name of my god be a father where there is no justice.
To mankind, the flock of the god Ner, whatever be their names,
    who are in field and city,
speak, O Sun-god, mighty lord, and bid the evil enchantment
    be at rest.'

Even the science of the Babylonians and their Assyrian disciples was not free from superstition. Astronomy
was mixed with astrology, and their observation of
terrestrial phenomena led only to an elaborate system
of augury. The false assumption was made that an
event was caused by another which had immediately
preceded it ; and hence it was laid down that whenever
two events had been observed to follow one upon the
other, the recurrence of the first would cause the other
to follow again. The assumption was an illustration of
the well-known fallacy: ' Post hoc, ergo propter hoc.
It produced both the pseudo-science of astrology and
the pseudo-science of augury.

The standard work on astronomy, as has already been
noted, was that called 'The Observations of Bel,' compiled originally for the library of Sargon I at Accad.
Additions were made to it from time to time, the chief
object of the work being to notice the events which
happened after each celestial phenomenon. Thus the
occurrences which at different periods followed a solar
eclipse on a particular day were all duly introduced
into the text and piled, as it were, one upon the other.
The table of contents prefixed to the work showed that

it treated of various matters  eclipses of the sun and
moon, the conjunction of the sun and moon, the phases
of Venus and Mars, the position of the pole star, the
changes of the weather, the appearance of comets, or, as
they are called, 'stars with a tail behind and a corona in
front,' and the like.   The immense collection of records
of eclipses indicates the length of time during which
observations of the heavens had been carried on.   As it
is generally stated whether a solar eclipse had happened
'according to calculation' or 'contrary to calculation,' it
is clear that the Babylonians were acquainted at an
early date with the periodicity of eclipses of the sun.
The beginning of the year was determined by the
position of the star Dilgan (α Aurigæ) in relation to
the new moon at the vernal equinox, and the night
was originally divided into three watches. Subsequently
the *kasbu* or 'double hour' was introduced to mark
time, twelve *kasbu* being equivalent to a night and day.
Time itself was measured by a clepsydra or water-clock,
as well as by a gnomon or dial.   The dial set up by
Ahaz at Jerusalem (2 Kings xx. 11) was doubtless one
of the fruits of his intercourse with the Assyrians.

The Zodiacal signs had been marked out and named
at that remote period when the sun was still in Taurus
at the beginning of spring, and the equator had been
divided into sixty degrees.   The year was correspondingly divided into twelve months, each of thirty days,
intercalary months being counted in by the priests when
necessary.   The British Museum possesses fragments of

a planisphere from Nineveh, representing the sky at the
time of the vernal equinox, the constellation of Tammuz or Orion being specially noticeable upon it.  Another
tablet contains a table of lunar longitudes.

With all this attention to astronomical matters it is
not surprising that every great city boasted of an
observatory, erected on the summit of a lofty tower.
Astronomers were appointed by the state to take charge
of these observatories, and to send in fortnightly reports
to the king.  Here are specimens of them, the first of
which is dated B.C. 649:—'To the king, my lord, thy
servant Istar-iddin-pal, one of the chief astronomers of
Arbela.  May there be peace to the king, my lord, may
Nebo, Merodach, and Istar of Arbela, be favourable to
the king, my lord.  On the twenty-ninth day we kept a
watch.  The observatory was covered with cloud : the
moon we did not see.  (Dated) the month Sebat, the
first day, the eponymy of Bel-kharran-Sadua.'  'To
the king, my lord, thy servant Abil-Istar.  May there
be peace to the king, my lord.  May Nebo and Merodach be propitious to the king, my lord.  May the great
gods grant unto the king, my lord, long days, soundness
of body, and joy of heart.  On the twenty-seventh day
(of the month) the moon disappeared.  On the twenty-
eighth, twenty-ninth, and thirtieth days, we kept a
watch for the eclipse of the sun.  But the sun did not
pass into eclipse.  On the first day the moon was seen
during the day.  During the month Tammuz (June) it
was above the planet Mercury, as I have already re-

ported to the king. During the period when the moon
is called Anu (*i.e.*, from the first to the fifth days of the
lunar month), it was seen declining in the orbit of
Arcturus. Owing to the rain the horn was not visible
Such is my report. During the period when the moon
was Anu, I sent to the king, my lord, the following
account of its conjunction:—It was stationary and
visible below the star of the chariot. During the period
when the moon is called Bel (*i.e.*, from the tenth to the
fifteenth day), it became full; to the star of the chariot
it approached. Its conjunction (with the star) was prevented; but its conjunction with Mercury, during the
period when it was Anu, of which I have already sent a
report to the king, my lord, was not prevented. May
the king, my lord, have peace!'

Astronomical observations imply a knowledge of
mathematics, and in this the Babylonians and Assyrians seem to have excelled. Tables of squares and
cubes have been found at Senkereh, the ancient Larsa,
and a series of geometrical figures used for augural
purposes presupposes a sort of Babylonian Euclid.
The mathematical unit was 60, which was understood
as a multiple when high numbers had to be expressed,
IV, for example, standing for ($4 \times 60 =$) 240. Similarly,
60 was the unwritten denominator of fractional numbers. The plan of an estate outside the gate of Zamama
at Babylon, and belonging to the time of Nebuchadnezzar, has been discovered, while the famous Hanging
Gardens of that city were watered by means of a screw.

Medicine also was in a more advanced state than might have been expected. Fragments of an old work on medicine have been found, which show that all known diseases had been classified, and their symptoms described, the medical mixtures considered appropriate to each being compounded and prescribed quite in modern fashion. Here is one of them : ' For a diseased gall-bladder, which devours the top of a man's heart like a ring (?) . . . within the sick (part), we prepare cypress-extract, goats' milk, palm-wine, barley, the flesh of an ox and bear, and the wine of the cellarer, in order that the sick man may live. Half an ephah of clear honey, half an ephah of cypress-extract, half an ephah of *gamgam* herbs, half an ephah of linseed, half an ephah of . . . , half an ephah of *imdi* herbs, half an ephah of the seed of *tarrati*, half an ephah of calves' milk, half an ephah of *senu* wood, half an ephah of *tik* powder, half an ephah of the . . . of the river-god, half an ephah of *usu* wood, half an ephah of mountain medicine, half an ephah of the flesh (?) of a dove, half an ephah of the seed of the . . , half an ephah of the corn of the field, ten measures of the juice of a cut herb, ten measures of the tooth of the sea (sea-weed), one ephah of putrid flesh (?), one ephah of dates, one ephah of palm-wine and *insik*, and one ephah of the flesh (?) of the entrails ; slice and cut up ; or mix as a mixture, after first stirring it with a reed. On the fourth day observe (the sick man's) countenance. If it shows a white appearance his heart is cured ; if it shows a dark appearance his heart is still devoured by the fire; if it shows a yellow appearance during the day, the patient's recovery is assured; if it shows a black appearance he will grow worse and will not live.   For the swelling (? , slice (the flesh of) a cow which has entered the stall and has been slaughtered during the day.   Seethe it in water and calves' milk. Drink the result in palm-wine.   Drink it during the day.'

Generally, however, the prescriptions are not so elaborate as this.   They are more usually of this nature: 'For low spirits, slice the root of the destiny tree, the root of the *susum* tree, two or three other vegetable compounds, and the tongue of a dog.   Drink the mix ture either in water or in palm-wine.'

Even medical science, however, was invaded by super- stition.   In place of trying the doctor's prescription, a patient often had the choice allowed him of having recourse to charms and exorcisms.   Thus the medical work itself permits him to 'place an incantation on the big toe of the left foot and cause it to remain' there, the incantation being as follows: 'O wind, my mother, wind, wind, the handmaid of the gods art thou; O wind among the storm-birds; yea, the water dost thou make stream down, and with the gods thy brothers liftest up the glory of thy wisdom.'   At other times a witch or sorceress was called in, and told to 'bind a cord twice seven times, binding it on the sick man's neck and on his feet like fetters, and while he lies in his bed to pour pure water over him.'   Instead of the knotted cord verses from a sacred book might be employed, just as phylacteries were, and still are, among the Jews.   Thus we read : 'In the night time let a verse from a good tablet be placed on the head of the sick man in bed.' The word translated 'verse' is *masal*, the Hebrew *mâshâl*, which literally signifies a 'proverb' or 'parable.' It is curious to find the witch by the side of the wizard in Babylonia.   'The wise woman,' however, was held in great repute there, and just as the witches of Europe were supposed to fly through the air on a broomstick so it was believed that the witches of Babylonia could perform the same feat with the help of a wooden staff.

## CHAPTER V.

MANNERS AND CUSTOMS; TRADE AND GOVERNMENT.

THE monuments of Assyria do not give us the same assistance as those of Egypt in learning about the manners and customs of its inhabitants. We find there no tombs whose pictured walls set before us the daily life and doings of the people. We have to acquire our knowledge from the bas-reliefs of the royal palaces, which represent to us rather the pomp of the court and the conquest of foreign nations than scenes taken from ordinary Assyrian life. It is only incidentally that the manners and customs of the lower classes are depicted. It is true that we can learn a good deal from the contract-tablets and other kinds of what may be called the private literature of Babylonia and Assyria. At present, however, but a small portion of these has been examined, and a literature can never paint so fully and distinctly the manners and customs of the day as the picture or sculpture on the wall. It is only in times comparatively modern that the novelist has sought to give a faithful portrait of the life of the peasant and artisan.

The dress of the upper classes in Assyria did not differ essentially from that of the well-to-do Oriental of to-day. In time of peace the king was dressed in a robe which reached to the ankles, bound round the waist with a broad belt, while a mantle was thrown over his shoulders, and a tiara or fillet was worn on his head. The tiara sometimes resembled the triple tiara of the Pope, sometimes was of cone-like shape, and the fillet was furnished with two long bandelettes which fell down behind. The robe and mantle were alike richly embroidered and edged with fringes. The arms were left bare, except in so far as they could be covered by the mantle, and a heavy pair of bracelets encircled each, the workmanship of the jewelry being similar to that of the chain which was worn round the neck. The feet were shod with sandals which had a raised part behind to protect the heels, and they were fastened to the feet by a ring through which the great toe passed, and a latchet over the instep. Sandals of precisely the same character are still used in Mesopotamia. The monarch's dress in war was similar to that used in time of peace, except that he carried a belt for daggers, while a fringed apron took the place of the mantle. Boots laced in front were also sometimes substituted for the sandals.

The upper classes, and more especially the officials about court, wore a costume similar to that of the king, only of course, less rich and costly. In all cases they were distinguished by the long fringed sleeveless robe which descended to the ankles. The dress of the soldiers and of the common people generally was quite different. It consisted only of the tunic, over which in

all probability the long robe of the wealthy was worn,
and which did not quite reach the knees.   Sometimes a
sort of jacket was put on above it, and, in a few
instances, a simple kilt seems to take its place.   The kilt
was frequently worn under the tunic, which was fastened
round the waist by a girdle or sword-belt.   The arms,
legs, and feet, were bare.   Some of the soldiers, however, wore sandals, and others, more particularly the
cavalry, wore boots, which were laced in front, and came
half way up the leg.   The upper part of the legs was
occasionally protected by drawers of leather or chain-
armour, and we even find tunics made of the same
materials.   Helmets were also employed, but the
common soldier usually covered his head with a simple
skull-cap.

The dress of the women consisted of a long tunic and
mantle, and a fillet for confining the hair.

The king and his officers rode in chariots even when
on a campaign.   In crossing mountains the chariots
often had to be carried on the shoulders of men or
animals, their wheels being sometimes first taken off for
the purpose.   The chariot was large enough to contain
not only the king but an umbrella-bearer and a cha-
rioteer as well.   The latter held the reins in both hands,
each rein being single and fastened to either side of a
snaffle-like bit.   When in the field the royal chariot was
followed by a bow-bearer and a quiver-bearer, as well
as by led horses, intended to assist the monarch to
escape, should the fortune of battle turn against him.

The chariot was drawn by two horses, a third horse being usually attached to it by a thong in order to

ASSYRIAN KING IN HIS CHARIOT.

take the place of one of the other two if an accident occurred.

Beside the chariots the army was accompanied by a corps of cavalry. In the time of the first Assyrian Empire the cavalry-soldier rode on the bare back of the horse, with his knees crouched up in front of him; subsequently saddles were introduced, though not stirrups.

The cavalry was divided into two corps—the heavy and the light-armed. The latter were armed only with the bow and arrow and a guard for the wrist, and were chiefly employed in skirmishing. Most of the archers, however, belonged to the infantry. The Assyrians were particularly skilled in the use of the bow, and their superiority in war was probably in great measure due to it. Besides the bow they employed the spear, the short dagger or dirk, and the sword, which was of two kinds. The ordinary kind was long and straight, the less usual kind being curved, like a scimetar. For defence, round shields, of no great size, were carried.

Only the king and the chief nobles were allowed the luxury of a tent. The common soldier had to sleep on the ground, wrapped up in a blanket or plaid. The tent was probably of felt, and had an opening in the centre through which the smoke of a fire might escape. Not only, however, was a sleeping-tent carried for the king, a cooking-tent was carried also. So also was the royal chair, called a *nimedu*, on which the monarch sat when stationary in camp. The chair may be seen in the bas-relief, now in the British Museum, which represents Sennacherib sitting upon it in front of the captured town of Lachish. Above is a short inscription which tells us that 'Sennacherib, the king of legions, the king of Assyria, sat on an upright throne, and the spoil of the city of Lachish passed before him.'

There were various means for assaulting a hostile town. Sometimes scaling-ladders were used, sometimes the walls were undermined with crowbars and pickaxes; sometimes a battering-ram was employed armed with one or two spear-like projections ; sometimes fire was applied to the enemy's gates. Other engines are men-

SIEGE OF A CITY.

tioned in the inscriptions, but as they have not been found depicted on the monuments it is difficult to identify them.

The barbarities which followed the capture of a town would be almost incredible, were they not a subject of boast in the inscriptions which record them. Assur-natsir-pal's cruelties were especially revolting. Pyramids of human heads marked the path of the conqueror ; boys and girls were burned alive or reserved for a worse fate ; men were impaled, flayed alive, blinded, or deprived of their hands and feet, of their ears and noses, while the women and children were carried into slavery, the captured city plundered and reduced to ashes, and the trees in its neighbourhood cut down. During the second Assyrian Empire warfare was a little more humane, but the most horrible tortures were still exer-

cised upon the vanquished.    How deeply-seated was the
thirst for blood and vengeance on an enemy is exempli-
fied in a bas-relief which represents Assur-bani-pal and
his queen feasting in their garden while the head of the
conquered Elamite king hangs from a tree above.

The Assyrians made use of chairs, tables, and couches.
A piece of sculpture from Khorsabad introduces us to
a scene in which the priests of the king are seated, two
on a chair on either side of a four-legged table.    Their
sandals are removed, as was the custom among the
Greeks when eating.    In the luxurious days of Assur-
bani-pal the couch seems to have partially taken the
place of the chair, since in the scene alluded to above
the king is depicted reclining, though the queen sits in a
chair by his side.    The number of different kinds of
food mentioned in the inscriptions seems to imply that
the Assyrians were fond of good living.    The common
people, it is true, lived mostly on bread, fruit, and vegetables ; but the monuments show us soldiers engaged in
slaughtering and cooking oxen and sheep.

Wine was the usual beverage at a banquet, and the
Assyrians appear to have resembled the Persians in
their indulgence in it.    Various sorts of wine are
enumerated in the inscriptions, most of which were
imported from abroad.    Among the most highly prized
was the wine of Khilbun or Helbon, which is mentioned
in Ezek. xxvii. 18, and was grown near Damascus at a
village still called Halbûn.    Besides grape-wine, palm-
wine, made from dates, was brought from Babylon, and

beer, milk, cream, butter or ghee, and oil, were all much used. At a feast the wine was ladled out of a large vase into cups, which were then presented to the guests.

The table was ornamented with flowers, and musicians were hired to amuse the banqueters. No less than seven or eight different musical instruments were known, among them the harp, the lyre, and the tambourine. The lyre seems to have been specially employed at feasts, and the harp for the performance of sacred music. The instrumental music was at times accompanied by the voice, and bands of musicians celebrated the triumphant return of the king from war.

Polygamy was permitted—at all events to the monarch —and the palace was accordingly guarded by a whole army of eunuchs. They were generally in attendance on the sovereign, like the scribes whose offices were continually needed in both peace and war. Another attendant must not be forgotten—the servant who stood behind the king armed with a fly-flap, and was almost a necessity in hot weather. Considering the number of captives carried away every year to Assyria in the successful campaigns of its rulers, slaves must have been very plentiful in Nineveh. Indeed, after the Arabian campaign of Assur-bani-pal we are told that a camel was sold for half a shekel of silver, and that a man was worth a correspondingly small sum.

Next to hunting men the chief employment and delight of an Assyrian king was to hunt wild beasts.

I

Tiglath-Pileser I had hunted elephants in the land of
the Hittites, as the Egyptian Pharaohs had done before
him; subsequently the extinction of the elephant in
Western Asia caused his successors to content themselves with lesser game. The reem or wild bull and the
lion became their favourite sport, smaller animals like
the gazelle, the hare, and the wild ass being left to their
subjects to pursue. It was not until the reign of Assur-
bani-pal that the lion-hunt ceased to be a dangerous and
exciting pastime. With Esar-haddon, however, the old
race of warrior kings had come to an end, and the new
king introduced a new style of sport. The lions were
now caught and kept in cages, until they were turned
out for a royal *battue*. As they had to be whipped into
activity, neither the monarch nor his companions could
have run much risk of being harmed.

The Assyrians were not an agricultural people like
the Babylonians. Nevertheless, the kings had their
paradises or parks, and the wealthier classes their
gardens or shrubberies. The garden was planted with
trees rather than with flowers or herbs, and afforded a
shady retreat during the summer months. Tiglath-
Pileser I had even established a sort of botanical garden,
in which he tried to acclimatise some of the trees he
had met with in his campaigns. He tells us of it: 'As
for the cedar, the *likkarin* tree, and the almug, from the
countries I have conquered, these trees, which none of
the kings my fathers that were before me had planted,
I took, and in the gardens of my land I planted, and by

the name of garden I called them; whatsoever in my
land there was not I took, and I established the gardens
of Assyria.' The gardens were abundantly watered
from the river or canal, by the side of which they were
usually planted. Summer-houses were built in the
midst of them, and as early as the time of Sennacherib
we meet with a 'hanging garden,' grown on the roof of
a building.

Fishing was carried on with a line merely, and without a rod. The fisherman sat on the bank, or else
swam in the water, supporting himself on an inflated
skin.

These inflated skins were largely used in warfare for
conveying troops and animals across a stream. The
chief officers, along with their chariots and commissariat,
were ferried across in boats, but the soldiers had to strip,
and with the help of the skins convey themselves, their
arms, the horses, and other baggage to the opposite
bank.

At times a pontoon-bridge of boats was constructed,
at other times the Assyrian army was fortunate enough
to meet with bridges of stone or wood. In fact, such
bridges existed on all the main roads which it traversed.
Western Asia was more thickly populated then than is
at present the case, and the roads were not only more
numerous than they are to-day, but better kept. Hence
the ease and rapidity with which large bodies of men
were moved by the Assyrian kings from one part of
Asia to another. Where a road did not already exist, it

was made by the advancing army, timber being cleared
and a highway thrown up for the purpose.

As road-makers the Assyrians seem to have antici-
pated the Romans.   Both their military and their
trading instincts led them in this direction.   It was only
when they came to the water that their career was
checked.   Excellent as they were as soldiers, they never
became sailors.   The boats of the Tigris and Euphrates
were either rafts or circular coracles of skins stretched
on a wooden framework.   When Sennacherib wished to
attack the Chaldeans of Bit-Yagina in their place of
refuge on the Persian Gulf, he had to transport Phœnicians from the west to build his galleys, and to navigate
them afterwards.   It was the Babylonians 'whose cry
was in their ships ; ' the Assyrians fought and traded on
shore.

It was not until the rise of the Second Assyrian
Empire that the trade of Assyria became important.
The earlier kings had gone forth to war for the sake of
booty or out of mere caprice ; Tiglath Pileser II and his
successors aimed at getting the commerce of the world
into the hands of their own subjects.   The fall of
Carchemish and the overthrow of the Phœnician cities
enabled them to carry out their design.   Nineveh
became a busy centre of trade, from whence caravans
went and returned north and south, east and west.
The old Hittite standard of weight, called 'the maneh
of Carchemish' by the Assyrians, was made the ordinary
legal standard, and Aramaic became the common lan-

guage of trade. Not unfrequently an Aramaic docket accompanies an Assyrian contract tablet, stating briefly what were its contents and the names of the chief contracting parties. These contract tablets have to do with the sale and lease of houses, slaves, and other property, as well as with the amount of interest to be paid upon loans. We learn from them that the rate of interest was usually as low as four per cent., and when objects like bronze were borrowed as three per cent. House property naturally varied in value. A house sold at Nineveh on the sixteenth of Sivan or May, B.C. 692, fetched one maneh of silver or £9, the average price of a slave. Thus, three Israelites, as Dr. Oppert believes, were sold by a Phœnician on the twentieth of Ab or July, B.C. 709, for £27, retractation or annulment of the sale being subject to a penalty of about £230, part of which was to go to the temple of Istar of Arbela. Twenty years later, however, as many as seven slaves, among them an Israelite, Hoshea, and his two wives, were sold for the same price, while we find a girl handed over by her parents to an Egyptian lady Nitôkris, who wished to marry her to her son Takhos, for the small sum of £2 10s. The last deed of sale, by the way, proves that wives in Assyria could sometimes be bought.

All deeds and contracts were signed and sealed in the presence of a number of attesting witnesses, who attached their seals, or, if they were too poor to possess any, their nail-marks, to the documents. It was then enclosed in an outer coating of clay, on which an abstract of its contents was given. Sometimes a further document on papyrus was fastened to it by means of a string.

It was only in the case of the monarch himself that the signatures of attesting witnesses were dispensed with. The British Museum possesses a sort of private will made by Sennacherib in favour of Esar-haddon, when the latter was not as yet heir-apparent to the throne. In this no witnesses are mentioned, and it is considered sufficient that the document should be lodged in the imperial archives. It runs as follows : 'I, Senna-cherib, king of legions, king of Assyria, bequeathe armlets of gold, quantities of ivory, a platter of gold, ornaments and chains for the neck, all these beautiful things of which there are heaps, and three sorts of pre-cious stones, $1\frac{1}{2}$ manehs and $2\frac{1}{2}$ shekels in weight, to Esar-haddon, my son, whose name was afterwards changed to Assur-sar-illik-pal by my wish. I have deposited the treasure in the house of Amuk. Thine is the kingdom, O Nebo, our light!' Payments, it must be remembered, were still made by weight, coined money not having been introduced until after the time of Nebuchadnezzar.

The business-like character of the trading community of Nineveh will best be gathered from the documents themselves which have been left to us. It will, there-fore, not be out of place to add here translations of some of the contract tablets :—

I. 'Ten shekels of the best silver for the head of Istar of Nineveh, which Bil lubaladh has lent on a loan in the presence of Mannu-ki-Arbela [here follow three seals]; the silver is to have interest paid upon it at four per cent. The silver has been given on the third day of the month. (Dated) the third day of Sebat, in the eponymy of Rimmon-lid-ani. The witnesses (are) Khatpi-sumnu, Rahu, Ziru-yukin, Neriglissor, Ebed-Nebo of Selappa, Musezib-Assur, Nebo-sallim-sunu, Khanni, and Bel-sad-ili.'

Then follow two lines and a half of Aramaic, the first of which contains the name of Mannu ki-Arbela.

II. 'Two talents of bronze, the property of Istar of Arbela, which Mannu-ki-Arbela gives to the goddess in the month Ab, in the presence of Samas-akhi-erba; if they are given, interest shall be paid on them at three per cent. (Dated) the eleventh day of Sivan, in the eponymy of Bamba (B.C. 676), before the witnesses: Istar-bab-esses, Kua, Sarru-ikbi, Dumku-pani-sarri, and Nebo-bilua.'

III. 'Four manehs of silver, according to the standard of Carchemish, which Neriglissor, in the presence of Nebo-sum-iddin, son of Nebo-rahim-baladhi, the superinten-dent of the Guards at Dur-Sargon (Khorsabad), lends out at five shekels of silver per month interest. (Dated) the twenty-sixth day of the month of Iyyar, in the eponymy of Gabbaru (B.C. 667). The witnesses are: Nebo-pal-iddin, Nebo-nirar, the holder of the two pens, Akhu-ramu of the same office, Assur-danin-sarri of the same office, Disi the astronomer, Samas igir sumeli (?), Sin kasid kala, the executioner, and Merodach . . . the astronomer.'

IV. 'The nail-mark of Sar-ludari, the nail-mark of Atar-suru, the nail-mark of the woman Amat-Suhla, the wife of Bel-dur, belonging to the third regiment, owners of the house which is sold. [Then follow four nail-marks.] The whole house, with its woodwork and its doors, situated in the city of Nineveh, adjoining the houses of Mannu-ki-akhi and El-kiya, near the markets (?), has been sold, and Tsil-Assur, the astrono-mer, an Egyptian, has received it for one maneh of silver, according to the royal standard (£9), in the presence of Sar-ludari, Atar-suru, and Amat-suhla, the wife of Bel-dur. The full price has been paid. This house has been bought. Withdrawal from the contract and agreement is forbidden. Whoever shall act fraudulently (?) at any time, or from among these men who have sworn to the contract and agreement with Tsil-Assur, shall be fined ten manehs of silver (£90). The witnesses are: Susanku-khatnanis, Khar-maza, the captain; Rasuh, the pilot; Nebo-dur-sanin, the foreign traveller; Kharmaza, the chief pilot; Sin-sar-utsur and Zedekiah. (Dated) the sixteenth day of Sivan, in the eponymy of Zaza (B.C. 692), the Governor of Arpad. In the presence of Samas-yukin-akhi, Latturu, and Nebo-sum-utsur.'

V. 'The seal of (Dagon-melech) the master of the slaves.—Imannu, the woman U . . . and Melech ur [Melchior], three persons, have been sold, and thou,

O Enuma-ili, the holder of the highplaces which have
been erected at the entrance to Dur Sargon, hast
received them from Dagon-melech for three manehs
of silver (£27) according to the standard of
Carchemish. The full price hast thou paid. These
slaves have been bought and taken. Withdrawal
from the contract and agreement is forbidden. Whoever shall act fraudulently (?) at any time, and shall
deceive and injure me (?), whether Dagon-melech or
his brothers, or the sons of his brothers, whether small
or great, who have sworn to the contract and agreement on behalf of Enuma-ili, his sons and grandsons,
shall pay . . (manehs) of silver, and one maneh of
gold to Istar of Arbela, and shall return the price to the
owners with ten per cent. interest. Then he will be
quit of his contract and agreement, and will not have
bought. The witnesses (are) : Adda the astronomer,
Akhu-irame the astronomer, Pakakha [Pekah] the
chief of the . . . , Nadbi-Yahu [Nadabiah] the
principal . . . Bel sime-ani, Bin-dikiri, Khim-Istar,
and Tabni the astronomer, the recipient of the
document. (Dated) the twentieth day of Ab, in the
eponymy of Mannu-ki Assur-lih ' (B.C. 709).

It will be noticed that the Israelitish witnesses to the
last deed of sale, Pekah and Nadabiah, hold public
offices, though the exact nature of them is at present
unknown. We may conclude from this that some of the
Samaritan captives were allowed to live in Nineveh, and
so far from being in a condition of slavery were able to

be in the service of the state. Among the earliest known examples of Israelitish or Jewish writing are seals which probably belong to a period anterior to the Babylonish Exile, and have been found at Diarbekr and other places in the neighbourhood of the Tigris and Euphrates. It is also possible that the great banking firm of Egibi, which flourished at Babylon from the time of Sennacherib and Esar-haddon to that of Darius and Xerxes, and carried on business transactions as extensive as those of the Rothschilds of to day, was of Israelitish origin. At all events the name Egibi is not Babylonian, while it is a very exact Babylonian transcript of the Biblical name Jacob.

The contract tablets throw a good deal of light upon Assyrian law. In its main outlines it did not differ much from our own. Precedents and previous decisions seem to have been held in as high estimation as among our own lawyers. The king was the supreme court of appeal, and copies exist of private petitions preferred to him on a variety of matters. Judges were appointed under the king, and prisons were established in the towns. An old Babylonian code of moral precepts addressed to princes denounces the ruler who listens to the evil advice of his courtiers, and does not deliver judgment 'according to the statutes,' 'the law-book,' and 'the writing of the god Ea.' The earliest existing code of laws is one which goes back to the Accadian epoch, and contains an express enactment for protecting the slave against his master. How far it was made the basis of subsequent Semitic legislation it is difficult to say; in one respect, at all events, it differed considerably from the law which followed it. This was in the position it assigned to women. Among the Accadians, the woman was the equal of man; in fact, she ranked before the husband in matters relating to the family; whereas among the Semites she was degraded to a very inferior rank. It is curious to find the Semitic translator of an Accadian text invariably changing the order in which the words for man and woman, male and female occur in the original. In the Accadian the order is 'woman and man,' in the Assyro-Babylonian translation, 'man and woman.'

The high-roads were placed under the charge of commissioners, and in Babylonia, where brick-making was an important occupation, the brick-yards as well. Certain of the taxes, which were raised alike from citizens and aliens, were devoted to the maintenance of them. Unfortunately we know but little at present of the precise way in which the taxes were levied, and the principle on which they were distributed among the various classes of the population. In Babylonia, how-ever, the tenant does not seem to have paid much to the government, since we are told of him that after handing over one-third of the produce of an estate to his landlord, he might keep the rest of it for himself. There is no hint that any portion of it was distrained for the state.

As in modern Turkey, the imperial exchequer after

the time of Tiglath-Pileser II was supplied by fixed contributions from the separate provinces and large towns. Thus Nineveh itself was assessed at thirty talents. The best way, however, of giving an idea of the assessment is by a translation of the few fragments of the assessment lists of the Second Empire which have been preserved to us.

I. 'To be expended on linen cloths. Fifty (talents).

Thirty talents. The tribute of Nineveh. Ten talents for firewood (?).

Twenty talents of Assyria, from the same city, for the equipment of the fleet.

Ten talents of Assyria, a fresh assessment. In all (from Assyria) 274 talents.

Twenty talents for the harem of the palace. Expended on linen cloths.

---

Five talents. The tribute of Calah. To be expended on firewood (?).

Four talents of Assyria, from the same city. Thirty talents for the highlands.

Ten talents from the city of Enil, for the lowlands.

. . . talents from the city of Nisibis. Twenty talents for 600 . . .

(. . . talents) from the city of Alikhu, for 600 dresses.

(. . . talents) for six vestures of linen. Three talents for *epâ*.

(. . . talents . . .) for keeping the gates in repair.

(. . . talents) for the tax-gatherer. Two talents from the city of Alikhu.

(. . . talents) for chariots and for wheels.

(. . . talents for the astronomer. Three talents for women's robes.

(. . . talents) for the throne of the palace in the middle of the city. Two talents for gala dresses.

(. . . talents) for the throne of the palace (in the middle of the city). Two talents ten manehs 500 (shekels).

. . . . . . in the city of Assur . . . again.

. . . . . . the city of Kalzu[1], two talents (for three conduits.

(. . . talents) from the city of Enil, for the persons of the overseers.

(Assessment of) the country of Assyria; two talents for the house of the tax-gatherer; two talents for the right side (of the house); five talents for the completion (of the assessment).

(. . . talents) from the nobles, and two talents from the librarians, for firewood (?) each year.

---

To be expended on linen cloths: ten talents from the land of Risu.

(For) the servants of the palace and the people of Nineveh.

---

. . . (for) seats, five talents from their attendants (Levied) every year from the lowlands.

---

[1] Now Shamameh, south-west Arbela.

The payment to be made by the tax-gatherer: two
talents for the male and female spinners.

———

(For) the house of the Master of the Singers: one
talent for their coverings.
Also for the house of the singing men themselves.
. . . for the keep of the war-chariot.   In all 190
talents ten manehs.

———

. . . manehs for his awning.   To be expended in
full.
. . . manehs for the broad streets of the public
road : seven talents ten manehs besides.
Forty manehs and a shekel and (?) a sleeved dress;
twenty-two talents for wood.
At six per cent. on each shekel let him put out the
money at triple interest.

———

Two talents without the linen.   Fifteen talents ten
manehs for the same personage.

———

Three talents ten  manehs for the custom-house.
Thirty talents ten manehs on (?) slaves.
Two manehs for wine presses.   The money to be put
out at double interest.

———

For rods : one talent (levied on) the north side (of
the city).   In all, twenty two talents to be invested.
Altogether thirty talents twenty-one manehs out of
fifty-three talents.

In the presence of the princes the money raised on the slaves to be invested.

---

[Here follows the endorsement of the tax-c llectors.]

We receive no bribes : we give what we take.'

II.  'Thirty talents (are annually received) from Arpad.

One hundred talents from Carchemish.

Thirty talents from the city of the Kuans.[1]

Fifteen talents from Megiddo.

Fifteen talents from Mannutsuate.

.  .  .   talents from Zemar (Gen. x. 18).

.  .  .   talents from Hadrach (Zech. ix. 1).

.      .     .     .     .     .?      .     .     .     .

.  .  .   talents to be put out at interest; fifty talents to be melted into bronze.

It is weighed in the presence of the princes.

(The tribute) of Damascus, Arpad, Carchemish, Kue, Tsubud, Zemar, and Meon Zemar.'

In spite of the fragmentary character of these lists, and the difficulty of understanding them perfectly in consequence of their brevity and the omission of prepositions, we may nevertheless glean from them a fair idea of the method in which the imperial exchequer of Assyria was replenished, and the objects to which the taxes and tribute were devoted. A considerable amount

---

[1] The Kue or Kuans inhabited the northern and eastern shores of the Gulf of Antioch.  M. François Lenormant has ingeniously suggested that in 1 Kings x. 28, we ought to read (with a slight change of vowel punctuation), 'And Solomon had horses brought out of Egypt, and out of Kue the king's merchants received a drove at a price.'

must have gone to the great army of officials by whom the Second Empire was administered. 'The great king,' it was true, was autocratic like the Russian Czar, but like the Russian Czar he was also controlled by a bureaucracy which managed the government under him. In military matters alone he was supreme, though even here two commanders in-chief stood at his side, ready to take his place in the command of the troops whenever age or disinclination detained him at home. The lists of Assyrian officials which we possess are very lengthy, and their titles seem almost endless. At the head came the two commanders-in-chief, the Turtannu or Tartan of the right, and the Turtannu of the left, doubtless so called from their position on the right and left of the king. Next to them were the Chamberlain or superintendent of the singing men and women, and then after five other officials whose posts are obscure, the 'Rab-sak' or 'Rab-shakeh.' His title means literally 'chief of the princes,' and he corresponded to the Vizier or Prime Minister of the Turkish Empire. Among other public offices we may notice that of the astronomer, who was supported by the state like the rest, and who ranked immediately after the 'superintendent of the camel-stables.' The latter again was inferior in rank to the 'captain of the watch,' 'the captain of fifty,' 'the overseer of the vineyards,' and 'the overseer of the quays.'

Such, then, was the constitution of the great Assyrian Empire, which first endeavoured to organise Western

Asia into a single homogeneous whole, and in effecting
its purpose cared neither for justice nor for humanity.
Nineveh was 'full of lies and robbery,' but it was God's
instrument in chastising His chosen people, and in pre-
paring the way for the ages that were to come, and for
a while, therefore, it was allowed to 'make the earth
empty' and 'waste.'   But the day came when its work
was accomplished, and the measure of its iniquity was
full.   Nineveh, 'the bloody city,' fell, never to rise again
and the doom pronounced by Nahum was fulfilled.   For
centuries the very site of the imperial city remained
unknown, and the traveller and historian alike put the
vain question : 'Where is the dwelling of the lions, and
the feeding-place of the young lions, where the lion,
even the old lion, walked, and the lion's whelp, and none
made them afraid ? '

# APPENDIX.

## Translations from Assyrian Texts relating to the History of the Kingdoms of Israel and Judah.

*From the inscription of Shalmaneser II, found at Kurkh, on the right bank of the Tigris, to the south-east of Diarbekr.*

' In the eponymy of Dayan-Assur (B.C. 854) on the 14th of the month Iyyar I left the city of Nineveh. The river Tigris I crossed. I approached the cities of Giammu on the river Balikh. The fear of my lordship, the sight of my strong weapons they feared, and in the service of themselves they slew Giammu their lord. I descended into the cities of Kitlala and Tul-sa-abil-akhi [the mound of the son of the brother] : I caused my gods to enter his palaces ; a plundering in his palaces I made. I opened his store chambers ; his treasures I seized. His goods, his spoil, I carried off ; to my city of Assur I brought (them). From the city of Kitlala I departed ; to the city of the Fort of Shalmaneser [Tul-Barsip, the Barsampsê of Ptolemy] I approached. In boats of inflated skins for the second time I crossed the Euphrates at its flood. The tribute of the kings of the further bank of the Euphrates ; of Sangar of Carchemish ; of Kundaspi of Komagênê : of Arame the son of Gusi ; of Lalli of Malatiyeh ; of Khayani, the son of Gabari ; of Girparuda of the Patinians ; and of Girparuda of the Gamgumians ; silver, gold, lead, bronze, and vases of bronze (in) the city of Assur-tamsukha-atsbat, on the further bank of the

Euphrates, and above the river Saguri [the Sajur]. which the Hittites call the city of Pethor, in the midst of it) I received. From the Euphrates I departed. The city of Khalman [Aleppo] I approached ; they feared battle ; they embraced my feet. Silver and gold I received as their tribute ; I offered sacrifices before the god Rimmon of Khalman. From the city of Khalman I departed ; to two cities of Irkhulena of Hamath I approached. The cities of Adennu [the Eden of Amos i 5], Barga and Argana his royal city I captured.[1] His spoil, his goods, and the treasures of his palaces I brought out. To his palaces I set fire. From the city of Argana I departed, the city of Karkar [Aroer] I approached. His) royal city of Karkar I threw down, dug up, and burned with fire. 1,200 chariots, 1,200 horsemen, and 20,000 men of Hadadezer of Damascus, 700 chariots, 700 horsemen, and 10,000 men of Ahab [Akhabbu] of Israel, 500 men of Kue, 1,000 men from Egypt, 10 chariots, and 10 000 men from the land of Irkanat, 200 men of Matinu-Baal of Arvad, 200 men from the land of Usanat, 30 chariots, and 10,000 men of Adon-Baal of Sizan, 1,000 camels of Gindibuh of the land of the Arabians [Arba'â], 200 men of Bahsa son of Rukhubi [Rehob] of Ammon, these twelve kings (Irkhulena) brought to his help, and to (make) war and battle against me they had come. With the exalted help which Assur the lord rendered, with the mighty weapons which the great protector who goes before me bestowed, I fought with them. From the city of Karkar to the city of Guzau I overthrew them. 14,000 of their troops I slew with weapons. Like Rimmon, the air-god, I caused the storm to come forth upon them. I filled the surface of the water with their (wrecks). I laid low their wide-spread forces with weapons. The low ground of the district received (?)

[1] On the bronze gates of Balawât Adennu is written Adâ and Barga Parga.

their corpses. To give life to its inhabitants I have enlarged its border (? ; that it might support them I divided (it among its people. The river Orontes I reached close to the banks. In the midst of this battle I took from them their chariots, their horsemen, their horses and their teams.'

### *From the Black Obelisk of Shalmaneser II.*

'In my eighteenth year for the sixteenth time I crossed the Euphrates. Hazael, of Damascus, advanced to battle; 1,121 of his chariots, 470 of his horsemen, along with his camp I took from him.'

### *From a Fragment of the Annals of Shalmaneser II.*

'In my eighteenth year for the sixteenth time I crossed the Euphrates. Hazael, of Damascus, trusted in the might of his army, and assembled his army without number. He made Mount Shenir, the highest peak of the mountains which are as you come to Mount Lebanon, his fortress I fought with him; I overthrew him; 16,000 of his fighting men I slew with weapons, 1,121 of his chariots, 470 of his horsemen, along with his camp, I took from him. To save his life he ascended (the country); I pursued after him. In Damascus, his royal city, I shut him up; his plantations I cut down. To the mountains of the Haurân I went; cities innumerable I threw down, I dug up, I burned with fire; their spoil innumerable I carried away. To the mountains of Baal-rosh at the promontory of the sea I went; I made an image of my majesty there. At that time I received the tribute of the Tyrians, of the Sidonians, and of Jehu, son of Omri.'

### *From the Inscription of Rimmon-nirari III.*

'Conqueror from the highroad of the rising sun, of the lands of Kip, Ellip [Ekbatana], Kharkhar, Arazias,

Mesu, the Medes, Girubbunda to its whole extent, Munna, Barsua, Allabria, Abdadana, Nahri to its extreme frontiers, and Andiu, whose situation is remote, the mountainous border land to its extreme frontiers, as far as the great sea of the rising sun [the Persian Gulf], from the Euphrates, and the lands of the Hittites, of Phœnicia to its whole extent, of Tyre, of Sidon, of Omri [Samaria], of Edom, and of Philistia as far as the great sea of the setting sun [the Mediterranean], to my yoke I subjected (them), payment of tribute I imposed upon them. To the land of Damascus I went; I shut up Marih, king of Syria, in Damascus, his royal city. The fear of the brilliance of Assur, his lord, overwhelmed him, and he took my feet; he offered homage. 2,300 talents of silver, 20 talents of gold, 3,000 talents of bronze, 5,000 talents of iron, garments of damask and linen, a couch of ivory, a sun-shade of ivory, I took, I carried to (Assyria). His spoil, his goods innumerable, I received in Damascus, his royal city, in the midst of his palace.'

*From Fragments of the Annals of Tiglath-Pileser II.*

I. 'They had embraced the mountain of Baal-tsephon [Mount Kasios] as far as the range of Amanus, the land of Zittu (?), the land of Sau to its whole extent, the province of the cities of Kar-Rimmon and Hadrach (Zech. ix. 1), the province of the city of Nukudina, the land of Khazu [Huz] as far as the cities in the circuit of the city of Arâ, the cities, all of them, the cities in their circuit, the mountain of Sarbua to its whole extent, the cities of Askhan and Yadab, Mount Yaraku to its whole extent, the cities of . . ri, Ellitarbi, and Zitânu as far as the midst of the city of Atinni . . . and the city of Buname, nineteen districts belonging to Hamath, together with the cities in their circuit in the direction of the sea of the setting sun [the Mediterranean], which in

their faithlessness made revolt to Azariah, I turned into
the territory of Assyria.   My governors and officers I
appointed over them.'

II. 'The tribute of Kustaspi of Komagênê, Rezon of
Damascus, Menahem of Samaria, Hiram of Tyre,
Sibitti-Baal of Gebal, Urikki of Kue, Pisiris of Carchemish, Eniel of Hamath, Parammu of Samahla,
Tarkhu-lara of Gamgum, Sulumal of Milid [Malatiyeh],
Dadilu of Kolkhis, Vas-surme of Tubal, Uskhitti of
Tuna, Urpalla of Tukhan, Tukhamme of Istunda,
Urimme of Khusimna, and Zabibieh, queen of the Arabians, gold, silver, lead, iron, elephants' hides, elephants'
tusks, tapestries of blue and purple, oak-wood, weapons
for service, a royal tent, sheep with bundles of their
wool, purple dye, the dyed feathers of flying birds, nine
of their wings coloured blue, horses, mules, oxen, sheep,
and wethers, camels and she-camels, together with their
young ones, I received.   In my ninth year Assur my
lord regarded me and to the countries of Kipsi, Irangi,
Tazakki, Media, Zualzas, Matti, and Umliyas I went.'

III. 'The towns of Gil ead and Abel-(beth-Maachah)
in the province of Beth-Omri [Samaria], the widespread
(district of Naphta)li to its whole extent I turned into
the territory of Assyria.   My (governors) and officers I
appointed (over them).   Khanun of Gaza who had fled
before my weapons escaped (to the land) of Egypt.   The
city of Gaza (his royal city I captured.   Its spoils), its
gods (I carried away.   My name) and the image of my
majesty (I set up) in the midst of the temple of  . . .
the gods of their land I counted (as a spoil) and  . . .
 . . . like a bird . . . . . . to his land I
restored him and (imposed tribute upon him.   Gold),
silver, garments of damask and linen (along with other
objects) I received.   The land of Beth-Omri  . . . .
a selection of its inhabitants (with their goods) I
transported to Assyria.   Pekah their king I put to death,
and I appointed Hosea to the sovereignty over them.

Ten (talents of gold, . . . of silver as) their tribute
I received, and I transported them (to Assyria).'

### *From the Inscriptions of Sargon.*

I. '(In the beginning of my reign) the city of Samaria
I besieged, I captured ; 27,280 of its inhabitants I
carried away ; fifty chariots in the midst of them I
collected, and the rest of their goods I seized ; I set my
governor over them and laid upon them the tribute of
the former king (Hosea).'

II. '(Sargon) the conqueror of the Thamudites, the
Ibadidites, the Marsimanites, and the Khapayans,[1] the
remainder of whom was carried away and whom he
transported to the midst of the land of Beth-Omri.'

III. 'The Thamudites, the (Ibadidites), the Marsimanites and the Khapayans, distant Arab tribes, who inhabit
the desert, of whom no scholar or envoy knew, and who
had never brought their tribute to the kings my (fathers),
I slaughtered in the service of Assur, and transported
what was left of them, setting them in the city of
Samaria.'

IV. '(In my ninth expedition and eleventh year) the
people of the Philistines, Judah, Edom and the Moabites
who dwell by the sea, who owed tribute and presents to
Assur my lord, plotted rebellion, men of insolence, who
in order to revolt against me carried their bribes for
alliance to Pharaoh king of Egypt, a prince who could
not save them, and sent him homage. I, Sargon, the
established prince, the reverer of the worship of Assur
and Merodach, the protector of the renown of Assur,
caused the warriors who belonged to me entirely to pass
the rivers Tigris and Euphrates during full flood, and
that same Yavan [of Ashdod], their king, who trusted in
his (forces), and did not (reverence) my sovereignty,
heard of the progress of my expedition to the land of

---

[1] Identified by Delitzsch with the Ephah of Gen. xxv. 4, and Is. lx. 6.

the Hittites [Syria], and the fear of (Assur) my (lord)
overwhelmed him, and to the border of Egypt . . .
he fled away.'

### From a Cylinder of Esar-haddon.

'I assembled the kings of Syria and the land beyond
the [Mediterranean] sea, Baal king of Tyre, Manasseh
king of Judah, Kaus-gabri king of Edom, Mizri[1] king of
Moab, Zil-Baal king of Gaza, Metinti king of Ashkelon,
Ikausu king of Ekron, Melech-asaph king of Gebal,
Matan-Baal king of Arvad, Abi-Baal king of Shamesh-
merom, Pedael king of Beth-Ammon, and Ahimelech
king of Ashdod, twelve kings of the sea-coast; Ekistor
king of Idalion, Pylagoras king of Khytros, Kissos
king of Salamis, Ithuander king of Paphos, Eriesos
king of Soloi, Damasos king of Kurion, Rumesu king
of Tamassos, Damusi king of Carthage, Unasagusu king
of Lidir, and Butsusu king of Nurê, ten kings of the
land of Cyprus in the middle of the sea.'

[1] That is 'the Egyptian;' cf. 2 Sam. xxiii, 20, 21.

# INDEX.

## A.

Accadians invented the cuneiform system of writing, founded the chief cities and civilisation of Babylonia; erected the earliest known monuments, the language may be called the Latin of Assyria, 24; the Accadians first used hieroglyphics or pictures painted n papyrus leaves, from which the cuneiform characters were formed; afterwards soft clay was stamped with cuneitic sym ls, and then sun-dried; general use of writing and materials em loyed; characters changed, 93 95; Sarzec's recent discovery at Tel-Loh, 95.

Adar, a solar deity; pronunciation of name not quite certain; it forms a part of the name Adrammelech, 66.

Adrammelech, one of the gods of Sepharvaim brought to Samaria by the colonists settled there; probably representing some par ticular attribute of the Sun god; also the name of one of Sennacherib's regicide sons, 46, 66.

Ahaz, king of Judah, called Jehoahaz in the inscriptions; bribed Pul to attack the Syrians and Israelites; and himself became tributary, 36.

Allat, the goddess queen of the underworld, 76.

APPENDIX.—Translations from Assyrian texts relating to the kingdoms of Israel and Judah:

I. Inscription of Shalmaneser II, found at Kurkh, 146-8.

II. The Black Obelisk of Shalmaneser II, 148.

III. From a Fragment of Shalmaneser II, 148.

IV. From the Inscription of Rimmon-nirari III, 148-9.

V. From Fragments of the Annals of Tiglath-Pileser II, 149 151

VI. From the Inscriptions of Sargon, 151 2.

VII. From a Cylinder of Esarhaddon, 152.

Aramaic, commonly used by the Jews, after the captivity, and ecame the c mmon language of trade, 132 3.

Ararat or Armenia, long a dangerous neighbour; Tiglath-Pileser II invaded the country, invested Van, and devastated the surrounding country, 35.

Armies composed of charioteers, light and heavy armed cavalry and infantry, and were variously equipped with bows, swords, and daggers, 126.

Armies cross ng streams; the common soldiers on inflated skins; the chief officers, chariots, and commissariat in b ats, or on pontoon bridges, 131.

Assessment lists of the provinces and large towns after the time of Tiglath-Pileser II; the places and amounts paid to the imperial exchequer, 140-3.

Assur, the name of a city on the western bank of the Tigris, and the capital of the country or district named after it; Assur was a

&c.; letters of the king, reports of astronomers and generals, 102.

Assyrian *palace*, built of brick on a raised platform; description, extent of courts and royal chambers; the observatory built in stages on the west side; exaggerated forms of columnar architecture used; apertures which served as windows protected in winter by heavy folds of tapestry, 86–8.

,, *sculptures*, mostly in relief; three periods traceable; characteristics and comparison with Egyptian art; colour used on the bas-reliefs, 89–90.

,, *Semites*, allied in blood and language to the Hebrews, Aramæans, and Arabs; the Babylonians a mixed race, partly Semites and Accadians, the original possessors of the soil of Chaldea, 24.

Assyrians and Babylonians contrasted, 66–7.

Assyro-Babylonians excelled in a knowledge of mathematics; tables of squares and cubes and geometrical figures have been found at Senkereh, and the plan of an estate at Babylon, 118.

## B.

Babel, tower of, and the dispersion, 82–3.

Babylonian *myth* of the seven evil spirits warring against the moon; flight of Samas and Istar; and the demons put to flight by Merodach; explanation of the myth, 78.

Babylonian *story* of the god Zu stealing the lightning of Bel compared with that of the Greek Prometheus, 78.

Balawât, colossal doors of, the work of native artists, description of the bronze framework and reliefs; explanatory texts relating to Shalmaneser's campaigns; Carchemish and Armenian warriors depicted, 30.

Banquets, wines of various kinds used; those of Helbon most highly prized; other luxuries common; the tables ornamented with flowers, and musicians hired to entertain the guests, 128–9.

Bel-kapkapi, the founder of the kingdom of Assur; its extent and varying frontiers; the inhabitants Semites, 27.

Bêrôssus' great work of seventy-two books translated into Greek, 102.

Blissful lot of the spirit of Ea-bani described in the epic of Gisdhubar, 76–7.

Botta and Layard's excavation brought to light Dur-Sargon and Nineveh, 26.

Bridges common on all the great roads through Western Asia in the earliest ages; used for war and trade; the country then more populous, and the roads numerous and well kept, 131–2.

## C.

Calah founded by Shalmaneser I, whose descendants reigned six generations; it became the seat of royalty under Assur-natsir-pal and Shalmaneser II, 27–9; the

## G.

Gisdhubar epic ; structure and contents ; each of its twelve books corresponded to one of the signs of the zodiac ; history of the Deluge contained in the eleventh book ; Gisdhubar a solar hero, and his adventures compared with the labours of Hêracles ; resemblance of Accadian and Greek myths ; date of the epic more than 2000 years before Christ ; formed of older lays put together to form a single poem, 110-12.

Goyim, over which Tidal was king, probably comprised in Gutium, or Kurdistan, 23.

## H.

Hadadezer (the Biblical Benhadad) of Damascus formed a confederacy with Hamath and Israel against the Assyrians ; Ahab's contingent ; rout f the allies at Karkar, or Aroer, 31.

Hades a dreary abode, where spirits flitted, like bats, among the crowned phantoms of heroes ; palace of Allat, where the waters of life, near the golden throne, restored to life and the upper air those who drank of them ; entrance, the River Datilla, 75 6.

Hanging gardens, watered by means of a screw, 118.

Hazael utterly routed by Shalmaneser II on the heights of Shenir ; camp, chariots, and carriages captured, and siege laid to Damascus, 31.

Helbon noted for its wines ; still called Halbûn, 127.

Highroads and brickyards placed under commissioners, 131 2.

Human sacrifices an Accadian institution ; children burnt to death as expiatory offerings by their fathers, 75.

Hymn to the Sun god, a mixture of exalted thought and debasing superstition, 113 5.

Hymns in honour of the different deities collected into a sacred book ; Semitic translations made, but the hymns recited long after war is in the original Accadian language, 67-8.

## I.

Inferior deities classed among ' the 300 spirits of heaven ' and ' the 600 spirits of earth,' 57.

Inscription containing Hezekiah's name transliterated and translated, 101 8.

Israelite officials witnesses of deed of sale, 137.

Istar the great Accadian goddess, unlike the Beltis or Bilat, wife of Baal, had independent attributes as strongly marked as those of the gods, and was known as the evening star, 57 ; she became the Semitic Ashtoreth, and was the goddess of love, war, and the chase ; she was associated with Tammuz ; her different attributes, temples, and worship in different places, 62-4.

## J.

Jehu's tribute to Shalmaneser II, gold and silver drinking vessels, a sceptre, and spear handles, 32.

Jewish seals probably earlier than the Babylonish exile found at Diarbekr and other places near the Tigris and Euphrates, 138.

carved on the rocky promont ry,
31-2; little further attempted y
the king, besides e\acting tribute
from distant regi ns; revolt of his
eldest son, j ined by twenty se\en
cities, put down by the energy and
military capacity of Samas-
Rimmon, 31 2.

Shalmaneser III, a usurper of Tinu;
he attempted the capture of Tyre,
began a war against Israel, but
had scarcely laid siege to Samaria
when he died or was murdered,
and was succeeded by Sargon,
another usurper, 37.

Sin, the Moon god, called Agu oi
Acu by the Acca lians, was the
patron deity of Ur; had a fam us
temple in the ancient city of
Harran, where he was symbolised
by an upright cone of stone; his
emblem was the crescent moon,
62.

## T.

Table of Semitic Babylonian kings
arranged in dynasties, which
traces them back to B.C. 2330; a
recent discovery, 102.

Tables of squares and cubes found
at Larsa, also geometrical figures
used for augury; the mathematical
unit, and mode of expression,
132 3.

Temple, Assyro Babylonian, and its
points of resemblance to Solomon's, 74 5; entrances to temples
and palaces guarded by col ssal
figures of winged bulls; temples
filled with images of the gods,
great and small, which were supposed to confer special sanctity
on the place; offerings of two
kinds, sacrifices and meal offerings; no traces of human sacrifices
among the Assyrians, although
an Accadian institution; referred
to in an old astrological work,

where children were allowe l to
be ffered by the fathers as expi
at ry sacrifices, 74 5.

Tiamat, the dragon, destroyed by
Merodach, 60, 78 9.

Tiglath-Pileser I, his conquests in
Cilicia, Kurdistan; defeated the
Moschi, Hittites, and their
Colchian allies, and erected a
memorial of his exploits near the
sources of the Tigris; he garri-
soned Pethor with Assyrian soldiers, and on his return to Nineveh
planted a park with strange trees
brought back with him during his
campaigns; he invaded Babylonia,
and was at first repulsed, but was
victorious afterwards, ravaged the
country, and captured Babylon,
28.

Tower of Babel, buil ling destroyed
by winds in the night, and 'great
and small,' as well as their
speech confounded by Anu, 82
3.

Trade, its rise and growth under
the Second Empire; fall of Carchemish and the Phœnician cities;
the standard of weight, 'the
maneh,' and Aramaic, the language of commerce, 132-3.

## V.

Van, the capital of Ararat, successfully resisted the Assyrians, whilst
the country far and near was
wasted for a space of 450 miles,
36; submitted to Sargon, and its
king Ursa committed suicide, 39;
Van sought an alliance with
Assur-bani pal, 52.

## W.

Witches and wizards held in high
repute, 121.

# INDEX OF SCRIPTURE REFERENCES.

HARRISON & SONS, Printers in Ordinary to Her Majesty, St. Martin's Lane.